# BROTHERHOOD PRIMER

## A MAN'S GUIDE TO TURNING BUDDIES INTO BROTHERS

### CHRIS BRUNO

Copyright © 2023 by Chris Bruno

All rights reserved.

No part of this book may be reproduced in any form or by any electronic or mechanical means, including information storage and retrieval systems, without written permission from the author, except for the use of brief quotations in a book review.

Restoration Project

155 West Harvard St STE 401

Fort Collins, CO 80525

ISBN 979-8-9877468-0-6

Cover design by: Cody Buriff, www.pinwheelcreative.net

All Scripture quotations, unless otherwise indicated, are taken from the HOLY BIBLE, NEW INTERNATIONAL VERSION®. NIV®. Copyright © 1973, 1978, 1984 by International Bible Society. Used by permission of Zondervan. All rights reserved worldwide.

Scripture quotations taken from the New American Standard NEW AMERICAN STANDARD BIBLE Copyright (C) 1960, 1962, 1963, 1968, 1971, 1972, 1973, 1975, 1977,1995 by THE LOCKMAN FOUNDATION Used by permission. All Rights Reserved http://www.lockman.org

# CONTENTS

1. Preparation: What I'm Talking About — 1
2. Manhood — 20
3. Brotherhood — 37
4. Space — 49
5. What Is Your Story? Part I — 66
6. What's Your Story? Part II — 86
7. How to Engage a Man's Story — 99
8. Pain — 114
9. Need — 132
10. Blessing — 143
    Epilogue: What's Next? — 155

Notes — 165
Introduction to Sage — 173
About the Author — 183

# 1
# PREPARATION: WHAT I'M TALKING ABOUT

This morning I woke up lonely. Not the kind of lonely where I'm convinced I don't have any friends. This kind of lonely feels like an ache in my gut telling me something is amiss. It's not an ache that tells me to lie down for a while or take a Tums. No, this is something far deeper, far closer to the core of who I am, what I'm about, and what it means for me to live the life God gave me. Something that is far more like a haunting than acid reflux.

This something is at the very center of every man's heart.[1] For some guys, even that word feels loaded–*heart*. It's come to mean that amorphous, touchy-feely thing that our post-modern, post-church society has robbed of all real grit. Whether you live in the inner city of Chicago, along the banks of the Mississippi, on Wall Street, on a houseboat in Seattle, or in the vastness of Wyoming, you still have it. Call it what you will–heart, gut, soul, being, center, life, core. They all mean the same thing, really. Let's just say that there's something there that aches. But for what?

If we're honest, it's an ache for other men. It took me several minutes to write that last sentence because it feels so weird to say out loud. We live in a culture that has ultimately demolished the notion of male-male relationship—either hyper-sexualizing it or completely belittling it (think *I Love You, Man*,[2] or the new term "man-date")—that we have lost any true sense of what it means to be close to another guy. The reality is, though, at the core of our beings as men is a hunger and need for other men.

We know it.

We feel it.

But we have lost the art of living as brothers.

And so we give in and settle for the relational table scraps of man-caves, touchdowns, Saturday morning church breakfasts, and over-the-fence backyard conversations, and we completely miss what God intended when he made men to be part of a "brotherhood."

## THE LAST SAUSAGE

Over the past 35 years, there has been a resurgence of interest in "man" things—masculinity, manhood, manliness, and what it means to "be a man" in the 21st century. Hundreds of sacred *and* secular organizations have sprung up to help guys "find themselves" in a variety of ways. The man-shelf at the bookstore grew exponentially over these decades, and a growing number of retreats, experiences, and offerings now provides men with more options to develop their masculine hearts. It is a good thing.

Many of these resources have been monumental in the lives of men. They have redirected wayward men, healed broken men, given hope to hopeless men, and restored shattered men. Some online content creators have set out to educate men in the art of being a man, including how to shave, dress, grout tile, sharpen knives, and skip a stone. We honestly can't complain about what good has come from the man-related industry as of late. These books, resources, and retreats have challenged us to do more than merely exist; they've given us a vision for what we could be.

But what about the ache? It's still there.

I was alone on an international flight recently with 16 hours to kill, a private television screen a mere 8 inches from my face, and an arsenal of movie selections at my fingertips. There are several films I would not watch at home with my wife simply because she does not like the war-themed plots or the gruesome battle scenes. It's fine. We watch other things. But if I'm honest, that's not the only reason I like these movies. Usually, in the foxholes and trenches of these epic tales, we find a brotherhood of men who battle together for a common cause. A deep camaraderie forms as they fight darkness, and while the film directors utilize the gruesome and the gory to cloak the deeper narrative, I believe men actually watch these movies for the bond rather than the battle. So, with hours and hours to kill on the flight, I settled in to absorb the unfolding brotherhood on screen.

I watched. I laughed. And I cried. Rather loudly, in fact, in the middle of the night at 35,000 feet over Greenland. I'm sure the woman in the burka a few seats over wondered what the flight attendant put in my drink.[3]

But then we landed, and I moved on.

Of course I did. When a man experiences something moving while he is alone, he shrugs it off or shuts it down and carries on. On the plane I experienced these courageous men in isolation, and as I emerged from the microcosm my headphones and seat 24C produced, I brushed off the emotion and stepped back into "reality." Who has friends like that anyway?

It's the same in the church. We are inundated with information. There is no lack of quality content readily available to us in a thousand different forms. From online sermons to podcasts, from inspirational speakers to seminary programs, from ebooks and Kindle to shelves and shelves of books at the store, we have more Christian information than we can possibly consume. And yet, transformation does not come from information. Transformation results from transformative relationships. And *that* is what this Brotherhood journey is all about.

The reality is that while we have a thousand resources to aid our hearts (or souls, or whatever you call it), a thousand movies to inspire us, a thousand men's breakfasts with a thousand speakers with predictable prayers, we simply move on. Yes, we might remember inklings, but like the smoke from a newly shot rifle, it dissipates the moment the wind blows through.

## IT'S ABOUT THE BUTTS

So then, what do we do? Is this what it means to be a man? Is this feeling of loneliness and lostness and dissipation the essence of my existence? Is this book just one more for the man-shelf?

Maybe.

In 2001, my wife and I bought new couches. It was a big deal. We had a baby, and the government decided we deserved an extra tax credit. So we cashed the check, passed "go," and hurried down to the furniture store. Married for six years[4] and in ministry, we'd never actually bought furniture at a store like real adults. Our little Michigan bungalow could barely hold the massive green couches the delivery truck left on our front porch. We would walk in the front door directly into the living room, and there they were. Couches everywhere. It was a bit much.

We kept those same couches for 12 years, 2 countries, 3 states, 5 homes, and 1 re-stuffing. We loved them. But the day came when we needed to say goodbye. Believe it or not, it felt like we were losing a part of our family, and we actually had a ceremony to commemorate their departure from our home.

What I realized about the couches is that they held *story*. The number of butts that sat on them is staggering. The gatherings, the tears, the laughter, the conflicts, the joys, the hard conversations, and even the empty conversations…all had meaning because of *who* the butts belonged to. Those butts belonged to people, and people have stories, and stories are what shape us all. You see, story is the currency of relationship.

I don't remember all of what was said, what was studied, what was learned, or what was revealed. But I do remember the companions along the journey called my life. Every single one of them. Life, real life, has little to do with content or information and far more to do with the narratives that shape and surround us. Connection to others, the kind of connection that attempts to take away the ache, happens when stories are told and held.

In *Tattoos on the Heart*,[5] Gregory Boyle quotes an African proverb that gives clarity to what *Brotherhood Primer* is all about: "A person becomes a person through other people."

Our *becoming* happens through other people.

And the people who have shaped me most have sat with me in the places where stories are shared. Not just "tell me about your vacation" types of stories, but the stories of victory and defeat, of pain and sorrow combined with relief and joy, of hope and fear and courage and terror. These are the stories and these are the relationships in which we are formed.

Half the butts on my couches through the years have belonged to valiant and beautiful women who have offered themselves with such stunning radiance that I can barely imagine life without their color. But this book is not about them or for them.

The other half have belonged to men. In my own life, and in the lives of hundreds of men whose butts have used my chairs, I see an even greater clarification of the African saying. If I may be so bold to modify ancient wisdom, I'd rephrase it to say: "A man becomes a man through other men." Like wet cement that is shaped and molded, I am convinced men become men by the presence and shaping of other men.

*That* is the ache. To become a man through other men requires other men, yet it takes intentional work for men to get there with each other. And then we get back into that whole weirdness thing, or we make attempts to be in the lives of other men and it just becomes about sin management and accountability, which is so much less than what God's design was ever meant to be. Or we may even have a season of great learning and openness, but we lose it when the winds change. As a result, we come to live with the ache like an old sports injury. We just assume it's part of life.

## BROTHERHOOD

But it's not. It's not meant to be part of life. That was never God's intent for men.

The word "brother" means far more than being born from the same parents.[6] To have a brother means you have a companion, a kinsman, an ally, a friend, of the same tribe and of the same purpose. To have a brother means you have a fellow journeyman through this life to shape and to sharpen, to witness each other's peaks and valleys, to disrupt you when you need disrupting, and to carry you when you can't make it on your own.

Brotherhood is another word for a man's becoming.

Brotherhood is synonymous to the holding of story and history in such a way that removes isolation, creates a context for connection, and allows men to enter one another's worlds without judgment, comparison, or competition. Brotherhood's focus is not on the content to be learned or the proper exegesis of a passage or on conformity to a certain ideology. Brotherhood's purpose is to know and be known by other men. For men to be "brothers," they know one another's depravity but hold fiercely and tightly to one another's glory in order to see each other become the men God intended for them to be. A brother is an ally of the Father on your behalf.

## BROTHERHOOD AND THE BIBLE

There is something about togetherness that God seems to enjoy. As a Triune God, where relationship is perfected between the Father, Son, and Spirit, He designed His image bearers on earth to know and experience companionship. Aloneness is antithetical to God's design.

The Bible is full of stories about brothers. And to be honest, their track record for having positive relationships isn't too good. Famous Bible brothers include Cain and Abel, Jacob and Esau, James and John (otherwise known as the "Sons of Thunder"), Joseph and his unhappy eleven brothers, and even Jesus's parable of the two brothers, to name but a few. Many of the brothers in the scriptures turn out to be archenemies. But I'm not talking about blood brothers who share DNA. I'm talking about *brotherhood*. Biological brothers are in relationship because they share parental origins. They had no choice in their earthly connection. But men choose to participate in brotherhood.

When we make this shift in understanding from *brothers* to *brotherhood*, we see a plethora of fantastic examples in the scriptures as well. Some of the most notable are David and Jonathan, Elijah and Elisha, Paul and Barnabas, Jesus and Peter, and James and John. Men choose to participate in brotherhood relationships out of an inherent need to be with other men. God did not design men to live in isolation.[7]

Consider even the incarnation of Jesus—the Son descending from heaven, taking on human flesh as a man, and coming to live on earth amongst his creation. The name "Emmanuel" means "God *with* us" and is a powerful reminder that God's heart for togetherness compels Him to step into human history in order to be our brother and friend. How is it that the God of all creation chose to walk amongst us? Even more stunning is the fact that He chose for Himself a brotherhood of men! Despite His participation in the Godhead, Jesus still wanted and needed to be surrounded by a close-knit group of other guys. Not because He had to, but because He chose to. He says, "I no longer call you servants....Instead, I have called you *friends*."[8]

If Jesus did it, then I supposed we should as well.

Brotherhood, in the end, is about being *with*. With is very different than "next to" or "doing the same activity." No, true *withness* is about entering into one another's lives in the places and ways that matter. *That* is the choice and motivation of brotherhood.

## THE ULTIMATE GOAL

I recently read a book about a completely different topic.[9] In it, the author made reference to some of the primary findings from men involved in the Promise Keepers' movement in the 1990s. The number one common thread of pain and loss among men: friendlessness. Number two: emotional isolation from other men. Number three: confusion about masculinity in the current cultural context. The list goes on and confirms over and over again the extreme need for men to relearn male-male relationality. We need it. We are desperate for it.

And yet the challenge is this: though we are lonely and isolated men, we do not have a roadmap to connecting with other men. Many of us were never taught how to step past the superficial into actual masculine relationships, having witnessed the anemic friendships of our fathers or experienced for ourselves the "man code" that discourages deeper emotional connection with other guys. Ultimately, my hope is that through the process laid out in *Brotherhood Primer* you will come a few steps closer to knowing and experiencing brotherhood with other men. I also believe God desires for all men to be part of an authentic brotherhood, and it is in this belief that I rest, knowing that hope can be a dangerous spark to ignite a powerful fire.

## NUTS AND BOLTS: HOW THIS WORKS

But this is not a book. It's a "primer." It's not designed to be a book that you read and think about by yourself in your quiet time, and then put away and move on. It's meant to prime the pump not just of your thinking, but of your actual brotherhood relationships. You can read all you want about becoming a brother, but until you *do it*–

engage other men's hearts; sit across from them and have that awkward moment of "I don't know what to do or say or think"; actually *do* brotherhood—it won't change a thing about you.

Remember, information does not change people. Relationships do. What I have provided here is meant to be a scaffolding and a catalyst to relationship. The most important content you bring to any brotherhood is not this book or anything I have to say. No, the most important content you can bring to other men is your own self with your own stories. *That* is the primary text.

Yes, you can read this book alone, but it is designed for you to engage alongside a small brotherhood of men. There are parts for you to consider alone, write down your thoughts, and reflect on your own life. However, the real grit and growth will occur as you take these reflections and offer them in trust to the other men you've gathered.

The first important step is to gather a group of men. These can be men you've known for a long time or men you met just last week. The important element is that these guys must have some desire for something more in their lives, both as individuals and, more importantly, in their relationships with other men. I recommend a group of 4 to 6 men. Any more, and it is easily sidetracked; any less, and it's just plain weird.

What are you asking them to do? This is a 10- to 16-week[10] primer designed to facilitate further personal exploration into what God is doing in your own manhood as well as to bring other men into authentic contact with your soul. This is __not__ an "accountability" group. It is __not__ a "Bible study" or a "men's group." This is a different animal. In essence, you are asking these guys to address the lack of depth in their current male-male friendships by seeking out more of God's design for life together with brothers along the way. Consider it an experiment.

Practically, you are asking them to walk through this primer with you, engaging their own stories and their own hearts along the way, while seeing what may develop between you as brothers. You are asking them to commit to reading the chapters, engaging the questions, and meeting together once a week.[11] Each week's Brotherhood gathering should be about an hour and a half. Start by doing one chapter per week. Then, when prompted, set aside several weeks for each man to share his story (much more detail on what that looks like in the upcoming chapters). After you finish this journey, it's up to you how you proceed. Again, this is designed to prime the pump, not be the pump.

While many guys like to gather at a restaurant or pub, I'd suggest avoiding those kinds of places for these meetings. It's just too loud and distracting, and you may be having conversations that you won't want overheard. Find a garage, basement, or backyard fire pit. I share more thoughts about the importance of this space in future chapters. For now, trust me.

Now I realize the bar is set pretty high. The greatest commodity for most men is their time. It's a lot to ask, but I am not going to apologize. The reality is we spend time, money, and energy on those things that are most valuable to us. Think about your commitment to the gym, to your career, to watching the evening news. You do it because you want it. You do it because it's important. There are plenty of barriers that prevent men from engaging in this kind of process with one another, the foremost likely being time. But I've kept the bar high because true brotherhood, when lived out over a lifetime, takes time and commitment. It's just a fact. If I lowered the bar, I'd be selling you a generic set of goods and training you to swim in the kiddie pool rather than setting your sights on the Olympic gold.

The reality is that each group will have a life of its own. God created each of you to participate in your own way and at this time of your life. Never before in history and never again will the uniqueness of your group occur. It's wonderful and curious and worthy of notice. The only thing you can control is the length of time you meet and how engaged you will be when you meet. Ultimately, it's up to you, your comrades, and the Spirit of God.

## GATHERING YOUR BROTHERHOOD

Probably the hardest part of this whole thing is gathering a group of guys to do this with you. You may already have a few in mind. You may be thumbing through your contact list hoping for a name or two to jump out at you. Either way, asking another guy to be involved in this kind of thing is nerve-racking. It just is.

First, pray. Ask God for direction in who to ask. Who are the men He's wanting you to pursue? I am convinced this is God's design for men. As a result, I believe it is His desire to provide every man with other men with whom to journey through this life. He's not holding out on you. Ask Him. Listen. Then ask them.

Second, have a "start date." Although the material starts off with content, I believe the best place to start with men is *play*. Invite the guys to some sort of gathering where you've got some good fun planned. Maybe it's a Scotch night around the fire pit. Maybe it's a poker night. Maybe it's a day of waterskiing on the lake. Maybe it's a hike or a shooting range. It doesn't matter as long as there is some sort of "intro" activity that gets the guys doing things together. It's vital to have a basis of relationship before diving into the categories of the heart. Your group may have a long history together, or you may be complete strangers. Either way, play is an essential place to start. Just think of it as loosening up the soil for the deeper things to come.

Third, discuss your commitment to the process at this initial gathering. It would be better to opt out before starting than to get involved and then have to back out in the middle. Can everyone create time to meet consistently and complete the individual work? We are all busy, and this primer requires a serious level of commitment—not to the primer, but to the other men in the group. Is every man willing to make sacrifices? Will everyone be at every gathering for the next 10 to 16 weeks? If not, can schedule modifications be made to accommodate?

Additionally, the primer will ask men to go to places personally and relationally they may be fearful and reticent to go. Is everyone willing to jump off that cliff, believing there is something more, something better? It is just plain awkward to be gathered with guys sharing their hearts and perspectives while one or two remain silent or distant. Will you be willing to step into the ring? Will you allow yourself to be challenged by the other men when they see you hiding in the bushes?

I have provided you with a **BROTHERHOOD COVENANT** and **RULES OF ENGAGEMENT** in the following pages. (You can also download the free pdf version at restorationproject.net/brotherhood. I highly recommend each man in the group to get his own copy.). The purpose is to formally agree together that you are committed to this process. I have found that men respond to a specific call. Rallying together around these basic agreements and covenants is a vital beginning to the shaping of your Brotherhood group.

Fourth, get the buy-in of your wife or significant other. If the guys are married or in a romantic relationship, it's important for their wives/girlfriends to be on board with this process. In one sense, these upcoming months will require time, energy, emotion, and focus from each man—meaning that he has to take this from somewhere. Ask each man to speak with his wife/girlfriend about what this could mean for him, for them, and for her. I am convinced that when men are *true men* as God intended, everyone benefits. The last thing a guy wants is to commit to a process like this and then have his wife/girlfriend either not understand, resent it, or undermine it in some way. Her buy-in is crucial.

Fifth, commit to an end. This is a 10- to 16-week primer. When will it be over? My goal is to help create relationships that will far outlive this process. However, at the end of the primer, it is best to reevaluate the relationships that have been built and give guys the "opt-out" option. Having that freedom of choice allows guys to dive more deeply into the process and avoid the feeling of being locked in for a lifetime.

Sixth, each man will need his own copy of *Brotherhood Primer*. Before the group's first gathering, make sure everyone has ample time to wander through the chapter titles, rhythms, and commitments.

And finally, start. Pray, pray, pray. Ask, ask, ask. Play, and then begin.

## A NOTE ON FACILITATING THE BROTHERHOOD

If you are the man giving leadership to this group, let me start by commending you. Well done. You have made a brave and bold step, one that I believe will cause goodness to ripple through the lives of families and communities for generations to come. I imagine the decision to start this journey comes out of both desire and past discouragement. By stepping into the ring, you are actively defying isolation, loneliness, and passivity. Thank you.

I've already said it, but I'll say it again. This is a different animal. Many of you may have experience leading small groups and accountability groups, facilitating meetings, or leading others in general. Your past experience will indeed be meaningful and helpful. Yet there are some significant differences between a typical church small group and what this primer seeks to achieve.

Ultimately, the key for the leader is to remember that the content provided in this book is far less important than the stories shared and the relationships built. There is no need to get all the questions asked and answered and no need to argue about the perspectives written. Of primary importance is how the individual men interact with their experience of being a man. My goal has been to provide a springboard for discussion, not to write "the absolute right way of being a man." Many will have different perspectives. Some will outright disagree with what I've written or proposed. As the facilitator, it is your role to make sure that the focus of the conversation during the gatherings is less about parsing words or making declarative, universal statements about manhood and more about *what we as men are learning about manhood from one another.* Remember, "men become men through other men."

Therefore, I've called it a "primer" for a reason: to prime the pump to get things flowing. The point is not the prime. The point is the well and the unique outflow that gets going as a result. Yes, there will be times when the facilitator will need to reorient and refocus the group toward the goal. But that goal is not the same as most content-based groups. The goal is to know and be known, not focus on the questions or the material.

> *The goal is to know and be known, not focus on the questions or the material.*

If you have chosen to gather and facilitate a group, I commend you for your courage, your tenacity, and your commitment both to your own soul as well as to the well-being of others. Maybe you are operating out of desperation. Maybe it's vision.

In the end, they are the same thing.

## QUESTIONS AS YOU BEGIN

Who will you gather? Write the names of the men you want to invite to be part of the Brotherhood. Aim for 4 to 6 men. No more than 6, no less than 4.

What day will your Brotherhood gather? What time? Where?

What will you do for your initial time together to get to know one another and have some fun?

What day will you all need to start reading/reflecting on the primer material in order to be ready for the first gathering?

## BROTHERHOOD COVENANT

A covenant is an agreement and commitment, a promise. For the Brotherhood process to be effective, all men need to be either fully in or fully out. Not in between. This is a rigorous process, and it is best for everyone to agree that he is *all in* before you begin. It's not signing your life away or making a long-term commitment to be part of the group beyond these 10 to 16 weeks, but it is stepping forward and making a promise that you will make the effort to fully participate in the process.

The men in this Brotherhood group include (maximum of 6 men):

Our Brotherhood gatherings will occur at __ am/pm at the following location:

We have agreed to meet on the following dates:


Confidentiality is an essential element to the development of any close relationship. You will be asked to investigate parts of your life and story as a man and to bring these reflections authentically to the others in your Brotherhood. You will not be coerced to share but challenged to go to new places in your own life and story, as well as in your relationships with other men. You agree to honor yourself and the other men by holding what is shared in this group in confidence. Confidence, or *con-fide,* means to have "faith with" others.

By signing below, I covenant with these men to complete the individual questions for each chapter, attend all gatherings, hold confidence, uphold the rules of engagement, and participate with as much authenticity as I can muster.

I have spoken with my wife or significant other, and she both understands the importance of this in my life and supports me as I pursue God's fullness for me in brotherhood with other men.

Signed:

## RULES OF ENGAGEMENT:

In order for this Brotherhood to work, we need to establish some basic Rules of Engagement. These are essential agreements that will help us stay on course and create an atmosphere that is safe, inviting, and encouraging. (Go to restorationproject.net/brotherhood to download this document for everyone to sign.)

**NO FIXING** | The intention of this type of group is to provide an environment where we do not seek to "fix" each other. A man needs the freedom to say what is on his mind and heart without the fear that others will want to placate, advise, or offer insight into what he should do. Everyone needs to agree to listen and not fix. Advice kills story. The only time advice is to be offered is if it is specifically invited.

**TIME IS CRUCIAL** | Time is one of men's most valuable assets. It is vitally important to respect one another's time. This means showing up on time and ending on time. If you would like to have additional time, go ahead...as long as it is agreed upon by all.

**STAY PRESENT** | You are in this to learn from and connect with one another. Therefore, you must all agree to engage one another from a place of curiosity rather than assumption. Additionally, it is important to stay engaged with the one talking rather than allow yourself to daydream or anticipate what you will say next. The ache men often feel is to know that others are truly "with" them when they are talking, not drifting away or jockeying for the next comment. Listen. Stay.

**SUSPEND JUDGMENT** | As this group gets going, you will likely encounter a variety of thoughts, lifestyles, opinions, theologies, and preferences that are vastly different from your own. This is not a place to correct or corral other men. It is, however, a place for you to consider other perspectives, other stories, and other ways of being. If you disagree with someone else's thoughts or choices, this is not the place to voice your concerns. This is a brotherhood, not a thought-police conference.

**RIGHTS AND WRONGS** | In order for an atmosphere of safety to be established, every man has the right to "pass" at any point. If he chooses to do so, the group should not push him. The only thing the group may ask is, "why?" It is wrong to force someone to talk about something that is too raw or vulnerable if he does not feel ready. It is better to stay in the group than to feel alienated and leave because of boundary violations.

**SHOW UP** | You will likely have to fight the urge to abandon the whole thing. Something may come up inside of you that does not want to take the risk to share. Shadows of fight or flight. Or maybe you will find yourself suddenly too tired to focus and engage. Or maybe you feel like what you shared was too much or too little and the other guys think you are an idiot. The most vital part of building relationships with other guys is consistently showing up and acknowledging those thoughts to them. In fact, one of the most transformational ways to deepen relationship with other men is to talk about how it feels to be in relationship with them. Share about your fears, your hopes, your anxieties, your shame. It will open the door to something far deeper than your silence ever could.

## PERSONAL REFLECTION

- First, go to RestorationProject.net/brotherhoodquiz and take the five-minute quiz to see what some of your core motivations are for saying "yes" to this group. The more you can understand your own desires and vision for this journey, and the more you share those with the men, the more likely it will be that you get what you came for. The results will be automatically emailed to you. Bring that email with you to the next group. The fact is, the results are secondary to the conversation that ensues as you collectively discuss your hopes for this gathering. Prior to that, spend a few minutes reflecting on these questions:
- How did those results land for you? What surprised you?
- In what way were you, or were you not, aware of your desires for this group?
- Why do you imagine the other men said "yes" to Brotherhood?
- Is there anything else you'd like to share with the men about your vision for this journey?

## GROUP DISCUSSION

- How did this introductory chapter hit you? What did you notice?
- What did you think about the results of the quiz? (If the men haven't taken the quiz, take five minutes and have the guys do the quiz.) How did you feel when you got your results?
- What were your results?
- As you read the Rules of Engagement, what are your thoughts? What excites you? What feels intimidating?

- Overall, how are you feeling about the process of going through this primer? Are you all in?
- (Take time, if you haven't already, to get schedules aligned and decide where you'll meet.)
- Pray for the coming weeks, for each other, and for yourselves.

# 2
# MANHOOD

The question of manhood and masculinity confronts us from every side. I don't know about you, but I have a pretty bad case of "manhood fatigue." According to several Super Bowl commercials, I'm a real man if I wear the right pants. Or drive the right car. Or visit Home Depot twice a week. I'm apparently a truly masculine man if I smell like a combination of sweat and ocean breeze and have bulging biceps and a skillfully shaped and well-oiled beard.

On the flip side, most television sitcoms actively make fun of men, depicting us as disengaged buffoons, violence and gore addicts, or sex-crazed and single-minded simpletons. Kitschy stores in tourist towns often have an ample supply of men-demeaning sayings imprinted on a variety of household items, such as "Don't ask me. I just live here," or "How to impress a woman: bend over and touch your toes, and while you are down there pick up your socks and underwear," or "A man is just a strategy for making other women," or "Men have feelings too. For example, hunger."

Even in the church, manhood messages abound. Depending on your tradition, real godly men either read their Bibles religiously or find creative alternative ways for spiritual expression. Real men hold on to tradition or real men break tradition. Real men either drink Scotch and smoke cigars or staunchly avoid them. It's all quite confusing, actually. One thing on which most Christian traditions can agree is that real men fly-fish.[1]

We live in a state of masculine crisis. More than ever before in the history of the world, what it means to be a man is unclear and in the crosshairs of society. Through the last century, stereotypes and social constructs of manhood have swung from hyper-independent and rugged individualism, depicted most acutely in John Wayne and the Marlboro Man, to the "free love" hippie with no responsibilities, to the sacrificial stay-at-home dad, to the toxic masculinity propagated by loud preachers who cannot get enough of themselves.

Manhood. The word is surrounded by landmines no matter where you go. And yet, now more than ever, I encounter guys who are desperate for thoughts and categories to help orient them to who they are, who God made them to be, and how to navigate the world *as a man*. I know I need this and so does my son. And the truth is, so do my wife and daughters.

Male. Man. Manhood. Masculinity. Some writers and scholars offer very precise and distinct definitions for each of these words, as well as female, woman, womanhood, and femininity. Clarifications of these can be helpful. But, for the sake of a more simplified discussion, I will be using these terms interchangeably. The one thing I would like to note for our discussion is this: I have put these words in a particular order, starting first with male because that is where every man begins. Then, a man who participates in a community of men is part of the greater collective known as manhood. And from that collective, we develop our understanding of masculinity. In the same way, a discussion about gender is beyond my hope for this chapter. Simpleton as I may seem, the discussion here will refer to gender in male/female, man/woman, manhood/womanhood, and masculine/feminine terms.

Similarly, femininity suffers its own gnarled mess of confusion.

Entire departments exist at universities with bachelor's, master's, and doctoral degrees in gender studies and feminist theory. Our world's messages to women are overwhelmingly conflicting. They are told to rise up, press in, and be strong, while simultaneously being objectified, diminished, and dismissed. A loud and bold man is considered confident and strong. A loud and bold woman is often viewed as a bitch. In one place women are encouraged to "free the nipple," while in another place they are forced to completely hide themselves from ever being seen or heard. The conundrum is confusing and exhausting.

As we enter into this intentional engagement of men around the concept of developing and deepening brotherhood with one another, our dialogue must start at the very beginning by attempting to answer the question: what makes us men? Now, there are far more intelligent, well-read, and articulate people in the world who are better qualified to provide a historical, sociological, biological, and spiritual answer to that question. I encourage you to more deeply investigate this inquiry beyond what I offer here. The truth is, in the midst of the chaos and confusion of our generation, we need more people to examine, understand, and clarify this question than ever before. Rather than cower from the task, be that person in your family, church, and community.

Recently, I was a guest on a podcast devoted to the clarification of masculinity for this generation. Throughout the interview, the host used language like "true masculinity," "traditional roles," "headship," "toxic," "provider," and referred to the glory of the past "when I was a boy." It made my head spin. You see, for several decades now (even centuries), we have been attempting to define masculinity from a sociological perspective, trying to moor ourselves to an ever-moving dock in the midst of a maelstrom. The primary reference point for manhood has been, by and large, either because of or in response to a patriarchal society. I do not find this helpful. We need a constant and reliable tether to an immovable and biblical pylon.

Therefore, I believe it goes back to humanity's origins in the Garden of Eden. It usually does.

It's really quite simple, actually. Whether it's society at large or the church, whether it's an African tribe or an American suburb, whether it's preteen or post-gen, there is one thing that stands as a universal signifier of manhood. And yet it seems the church (and society for that matter) woefully prepares us for this answer.

The universal signifier that an individual is male is a penis.

Even before a newborn infant takes its first wailing breath, doctors and nurses and eager parents zero in on that tender spot between the legs. Is there one, or is there not? Humans with this external member are male and will develop into men. It's just a fact. Now, having one or having a different set of marvelous organs has no bearing on the *value* of the individual.[2] But the existence of a penis inherently identifies God's design and direction for this person to grow up into a man.[3]

In Abigail Favale's fascinating book, *The Genesis of Gender: A Christian Theory*, she provides one of the most brilliantly profound and yet simple foundations for maleness and femaleness I have ever read. She writes:

> "Human bodies are teleologically organized according to our distinct role in reproducing the species. The structure of our bodies is arranged to produce either large sex cells or small sex cells. These sex cells are called gametes. Large gametes are ova, and small gametes are sperm. A physiology arranged to produce ova is female, and a physiology arranged to produce sperm is male. This twofold distinction between large and small gametes is stable and universal, not only throughout the human species, but also among *all* plant and animal species that reproduce sexually."[4]

To discover maleness or femaleness in the human body, we investigate how it is reproductively organized. Sperm producers are male, and ova producers are female. Additionally, if it is designed to reproduce life in another, it is male. If it is designed to gestate life within itself, it is female.[5]

By now I'm sure this is more than you bargained for when you picked up a book on brotherhood. My hope here is to provide you and your brothers a common foundation on which to build your connection to one another. Though men come in all shapes and sizes, from all cultures, races, and backgrounds, from all creeds, political affiliations, and personalities, we have one very important commonality that unites us all. Penises.[6]

Years ago I spoke at a church function with a crowd of 40 or so men. I had been asked to address the spiritual process of becoming godly men. As you might expect, even in the context of a men's gathering, there stands a tremendous reticence to using the word "penis." It's just not done. It's not civilized or righteous or whatever. But as I began to speak, I repeatedly and intentionally used the word "penis" in a variety of ways. I'm sure even now some of you are either smiling or cringing as you read.[7] In fact, say it out loud right now. See how it feels just to say the word. We just don't talk about penises without some sense of shame or the need to cover up our shame with humor or laughter. Penis-talk feels like it should have been left back in middle school.

But it's true. What indicates you are a man? Answer: your penis.[8]

So, what's my point? No, it's not just because I like typing or saying that word (though it never fails to result in someone blushing). The truth is that God's design for men *as men* harkens back to his original design—a *gendered* plan from the beginning that organizes and informs every cell of our being and is most clearly manifested in what dangles between our legs.[9]

I'm not trying to be crude. Really, I'm not. I've probably put off a good number of you by now because it's just not "Christian" to talk about genitals or gender. But in reality, our desire to discover our manhood is not distant or high and lofty and extremely difficult to understand or attain. No, a deeper understanding of our manhood is best gained by *how* God made us and *why* He made us the way He did. It was no mistake.

## ZAKAR AND NEQEBAH

Read Genesis 1:26-27.

> "Then God said, 'Let us make *mankind* in our image, in our likeness, so that they may rule over the fish in the sea and the birds in the sky, over the livestock and all the wild animals, and over all the creatures that move along the ground.'
>
> So God created *mankind* in His image,
> in the image of God He created them;
> *male* and *female* He created them."[10]

In the Genesis account of creation, we have an amazingly poetic explanation of the Earth's first days. The first three chapters of the scriptures establish a remarkable backdrop to the entire human story—or rather, God's story that includes us people. Whatever your beliefs are around the actual events of creation, you have to admit, these chapters provide a deep and profound understanding of the human condition.

Throughout the scriptures there are several words that have similar but distinctly different meanings. Translators have done their best to provide us with good English alternatives; however, every person who speaks two or more languages knows that some words just don't translate well or easily. For example, one of the more well-known multi-meaning words is the English word for "love." Greek has five different words for love,[11] all with significantly different nuances and meanings. In these Genesis verses, we find two Hebrew words that may seem similar, but they had immensely different implications to the original audience.

The first is the word "mankind." In Hebrew, this is the word *adam*, from which we get the first man's name, Adam. This word is a signifier to both the individual person and the race he represents, or all of humanity. After creating the world and all the animals, God decides He needs an ambassadorial race to stand as steward over His creation.[12] He creates them "in His likeness" or "in His image," in order for all creation to remember *Him* when they look at *them*. There is to be a family resemblance.

In verse 1:27, the writer heightens the importance of gender even more by setting it even further apart in the creation account. Twice in these few short verses we see that God creates humanity in His image, employing the poetic device of repetition, which signifies great importance. Then, as if linguistically and artfully set on a verbal pedestal, two new words appear, two words never before mentioned in all of the previous verses of the creation account. These words are "*male* and *female*."

I know that doesn't seem like a game stopper, but take a moment and think about it. For the previous 5 days and 25 verses, God created all sorts of creatures in all sorts of places—in the air, earth, and water. He crafted and shaped everything from frogs to bears to seagulls to sharks to Chihuahuas, and in the process he told them to "be fruitful and multiply." Now, any seventh grade biology class will tell you what that means. These animals had the proper sexual equipment in order to reproduce in their own unique ways. Their mutual reproductive organization allowed and compelled them to make more of themselves. This means that along the way, God gave them male parts and female parts in order to do as He commanded.

So what's the big deal? When God decided that humans are a good idea and that they should be made in His image, He not only states that He made *adam*, His race of representatives, but that He made them *male* and *female*. Never before in the creation account has this clarification been made. The distinction of gender, the identification and clarification of male and female, is only made in relation to humans. It's so important, if you jump a few chapters forward, you see it once more. In Genesis 5:2, we read: "When God created mankind [*adam*], He made them in the likeness of God. He created them male [*zakar*] and female [*neqebah*] and blessed them. And He named them 'Mankind' [*adam*] when they were created." Linked to the image of God in humanity is this notion of *male* and *female*. It's almost as if He wants us to know that there is something more to who we are by how we are made.

The one God images Himself into two humans as male and female.

So, what does this mean? What is God trying to communicate to us about our origins and meaning? This is where it gets interesting.

**MALE = ZAKAR**

In Hebrew, the word for "male" is *zakar*. Its most primary meaning is a direct reference to the phallus. It literally means "the one who pierces, sharp." Connoted in the word are aspects of being sometimes tender and soft, sometimes hard and rigid. There is a sense of prominence, reaching out, extending, or protruding. *Zakar* brings with it a piercing-ness through which life is delivered. In addition, there is a connotation of action, of stepping out and moving in. *Zakar* is not passive. Could it be any clearer that this is a direct reference to the penis? In fact, in many ancient languages still spoken today, such as Arabic, Farsi, and Hebrew, the word carries the same meaning.[13]

**FEMALE = NEQEBAH**

*Neqebah*, in turn, means "the one who is pierced" and carries the nurturing connotations of the womb. It has a sense of suppleness, openness, receiving, and care. The essence of the piercing is not violence, but receptivity and longing. For the woman, *neqebah* exudes vulnerability and trust, in which she opens and receives. Do you see the anatomical connections there as well? It becomes the term for "woman" and again is carried forth in modern use to this day.[14]

From the very beginning, we see a direct connection between God's image and our anatomy: to pierce and to be pierced. God is intent on making the correlation between *who we are* and *what we have*. Both men and women bear His image and walk in His likeness, each uniquely as male and female. It is as if He took His image and split it in two, creating a connected yet necessary dichotomy of identity. On the one hand, He is tender and vulnerable while also being occasionally powerful, piercing, strong, and hard. On the other hand, He is welcoming and receiving while also nurturing and creative. In a beautiful combination of character and anatomy, He crafted men to be men and women to be women. This is not to say that men are not or should not be gentle and nurturing or that women are not also strong and powerful. But this display of His likeness gives depth of insight into the character and nature of what it means to be *gendered*.

Briefly consider a short theology found in Psalm 62. Here the Psalmist says, "One thing God has spoken, two things I have heard: 'Power belongs to you, God, and with you, Lord, is unfailing love.'"[15] In the very character of God reside these two aspects of power and love. Other versions translate these words as strength and tenderness, or strength and lovingkindness. Remarkably, the character of God manifests these two very different aspects with harmonious perfection. And yet in the duality of His creation, male and female, He has endowed one with an ability to lengthen, extend, and harden, and the other with the ability to stretch and lovingly generate life. In all of this, it goes far beyond sexuality and into the very nature of what it means to be male and female. Each has a special way of reflecting and representing the King.[16]

And all of this is found in the first few verses of Genesis. As I said, it really does go back to the Garden. "Male and female He created them." Penis and vagina. Strong and tender. Piercer and pierced one.

Yet culture today brings the question of manhood into such confusion when in reality it is quite simple. What qualifies an individual to be a man, to be a masculine image bearer of God? If you are ever in question, the Bible invites you to look in your shorts. In those moments when you ask, "Do I have what it takes?" or "Am I man enough?" or "Can I truly be a man?" the answer is surprisingly simple. According to the scriptures, it's pretty clear. If you have a penis, you are a man. God designed *your manhood* when He designed you, and He put everything you need to be that man within you. That's it.

> *God designed your manhood when he designed you, and he put everything you need to be that man within you.*

Rather than embark on a lifelong search for more information about what manhood truly is or means, it is my hope to turn you toward your Maker. Manhood is not something to be found or attained as if it were buried under the X on a treasure map. God did not equip you to be a man *physically* without also endowing you with the right equipment *internally*–spiritually, emotionally, or soulfully. And just as He made you unique amongst all the other eight billion people who populate the planet, your manhood will also be unique–similar to other men, but unique. Your manhood is different from mine, though categorically we are alike. Yet so much of our modern-day manhood talk attempts to define and constrain and corral us toward a narrow understanding and definition. While there are aspects of our manhood that get bent, buried, and marred, the truth is that your God-designed manhood is already there, *in you*. If God began something in you, is He not faithful to carry it on and complete it also?[17]

The reality is we have lost the way to our own selves because we have lost our guides. Over the last century, boys have increasingly had to find their own way as men in the world. After the industrial revolution, boys[18] lost their fathers to factories and work. Women, amazing and blessedly gifted as they are, ended up holding the responsibility of raising boys into men. Without the intentionality of the father, boys relied on *neqebah* to find their way toward their *zakar*. Boys cannot be guided into manhood by a woman any more than a woman can describe the intensity of labor pains to a man. You can get close but not hit it fully. The reality is that boys are born, but men are made. A man becomes a man through other men. And when there are no men to make boys into men, whole generations of men are lost without their manhood bearings. Throw in there a national economic depression, a few world wars, and an emerging global superpower that rewarded fathers for their devotion to work, and the net result is a gaping black hole of masculine understanding.[19]

As a counselor of men, I hear it all. Sam, an artist in his early twenties on the West Coast, asked me, "What does it mean for me to be a man?" Carl, an ex-worship leader in his mid-thirties from Texas, after losing his career as a musician to a tragic spinal cord injury in a skiing accident, asked, "What do I do now? Will I ever be a man again?" Ben, a thirty-something inner-city minister to gangs in Chicago, commented, "After finding out about the violence between my father and mother, I'm not sure where to turn. I'm getting anxious that my book contract won't come through. There are so many other guys my age who are published already. I just don't measure up." Each of these men, and countless others, longs for a sense of himself and has been told that he must rely *on himself* to find his way. It's just not how it was supposed to be.

In the end, rather than embarking on a journey to a distant summit to find your manhood, I believe God is calling you to consider who and how He's already made you. It's not an outward quest, but an inward one.

## WHY IS THIS IMPORTANT?

So after all of that, what's the big deal? What does this have to do with brotherhood?

When my kids were younger, we hosted an after-season party for my daughter's soccer team. All the families were invited, resulting in roughly 25 children and 10 adults swarming my house and backyard.

Most of the mothers knew one another from school or sideline chatter. They gathered in a huddle and commenced conversation.

The men, mostly only acquaintances, stood somewhat awkwardly around the grill as I attempted to keep the hot dogs and brats from scorching. You can imagine the scene and anticipate the questions: What do you do? Where do you work? How long have you lived here? Cursory inquiries looking for some kernel of connection to break the silence.

Most of a man's world revolves around what he *does* or *knows*. These surface-level questions garner information about a man by discovering how he fills his time. We've been raised to believe for a man to truly be a man, his time must be full. How many times this last week did you ask someone, "How are you?" only to be met with the answer, "Busy. Tired." How often was that your answer as well? The modern-day measure of a man seems to be found on the metric of his exhaustion.

The thing is, culture also tells us that manhood is a moving target. It's more of a club, really. It all depends on the newest model phone, pocketknife, or SUV. Buy the right one, and you're in the club. If it's not that, it's all about your *score*—your bench-press score, your bank account score, your handsome score, your wife's beauty score, your bed score, and, most definitely, your busy score. It has little to do with what is already within.

In many ways, the church plays along and tells us that manhood is something to be attained and that strict accountability or mountaintop experiences will bring you one step closer to authentic manhood. We have to overcome something in us, we must tame our inner dragons, before we can consider ourselves to be true men. We are taught that manhood is measured by task and spiritual busyness. The journey toward manhood involves immense amounts of time, devotion, discipline, prayer, and doing. Manhood is somewhere "out there," and we are to try hard to find it. I know many men who struggle with guilt every time they miss a men's meeting, a men's breakfast, or a men's devotion time. On the path toward manhood, they have in some way fallen off the wagon and should be admonished back into line. Modern-day Christian manhood is always just out of reach.[20]

The scriptures, on the other hand, indicate otherwise.

Rather than striving toward the unreachable summit called "manhood," every man can rest assured–God has already granted it to you. It's inherently in you. Yes, it may need to be uncovered, refined, or better understood. But no man will acquire manhood through doing or knowing. He must discover it within himself, and then he can more deeply comprehend it through connection with other men. Sam, Carl, and Ben need a brotherhood. They don't need content. They don't need a method. They don't need information. What they need is other men to reflect back to them the manhood already there. But to say so feels as vulnerable as inviting a bowling ball to the groin.

Look around you. Are there men? There should be, because we make up roughly 50% of the population. And while I understand you might not want a deep and lasting friendship with every man around you, God has surrounded you with men. Their experience of being a man may be scarily similar to yours or vastly different. But the point is that there is something about manhood that they have and you need, and vice versa, just by being male. The connection is that you both own the right equipment, and somewhere embedded in your maleness is the image of God. *That's* what we're after.

Brotherhood, therefore, is an acknowledgement of sameness from one man to another, stating that *we have an inherent connection* just by being men. It is coming alongside one another in the pursuit of God, ourselves, and the other, recognizing that though we are different, we are the same. To be a brother means far more than having someone with whom I hang out or watch the game. To be a brother means that we live this life together as male image bearers. You help me understand myself, and I help you understand yourself. We have the same lenses through which we view life, and although there may be a million different tints to those shades, the glasses are the same.

The more I know my brothers, the more I know myself and the more I catch a glimpse of the Creator God. Men long for connection with one another because we long to know the God who made us men. We've just lost touch with how to get there.

## WHAT THIS IS NOT ABOUT

This primer is therefore not about giving you the tools, techniques, and information that will help you arrive at a better sense of manhood or masculinity. I don't have 10 steps or 5 processes or even 3 great ideas.

My hope in this work is to "prime the pump" in connections and relationships between men so you may journey together through this life as men. I don't have the answers, but you do. You will discover the uniqueness of who God created you to be as a man in the company of other men. At the end of this journey, you may not be closer to "authentic manhood" (whatever that means) than when you began, but you will have a deeper understanding of what it means to be *brothers* and, hopefully, a deeper sense of what it means to be the man God made you to be. It is as you bring yourself to interact authentically and vulnerably with other men that you will find natural connections and understandings emerging. You will have to push through aspects of engagement with other men that may, at first, be new. It is your choice to stay standing awkwardly around the grill with nothing but surface questions or to dive deeper into new ways of interaction that open up friendships with other men on a completely different level.

Neither the church nor society has provided us with the perspectives or the tools to pursue deeper male-male relationships that are genuine. We just don't know how. As a result, the content here is meant to be a catalyst toward personal reflection, disruption, and reorientation. It is designed to provide your Brotherhood group with some meat to chew on together. The actual content is far less important than your personal and corporate engagement with it and one another. It is meant as a doorway to conversation and much more. My hope is to create a space where men are pursuing the hearts, minds, souls, and stories of other men. If I can help a group of acquaintances take one step closer to being brothers, I have succeeded.

Every man, that is, every penis owner, has already been granted his manhood. You are *zakar*. In order to live into that manhood, the most important thing you need is brothers *because men become men through other men*.

## PERSONAL REFLECTION

- What are your hopes for this Brotherhood experience? What do you want to see happen <u>for you</u> through the next couple of months?
- What are your hesitations and fears of what this will be like?
- What do you think the other guys are thinking?
- How do you react to the *zakar* discussion?
- In your experience of your own manhood, where have you been emasculated? (How have you been told you are either not enough or too dangerous?)
- When you think about the other men in your group, how are you comparing yourself to them? Who is the bigger/better man? How do you tend to measure how you fit in?
- How do you sense yourself preparing to protect yourself as the gathering draws near?

## GROUP DISCUSSION

- Why did you say yes to this group? What do you hope to get out of this?
- What has been your experience of male friendships in the past? Good? Bad? Neutral?
- What do you make of the pursuit of manhood our culture and churches promote? Where are you in the process?
- What were your reactions to the *zakar* material? How comfortable are you with the notion that the image of God resides in your manhood?
- What are your fears as you dive into this group?
- In what ways do you see your defenses up even now in this group? What are you defending against? What are

you wanting to keep hidden? *(This is not a bare-your-soul kind of question, asking you to share your deepest, darkest secrets. Rather, what part of your heart/soul are you afraid other men will misunderstand or mistreat?)*
- Why do *you* need brothers?
- How do other men confirm or threaten your sense of masculinity? How do you compare yourself to other men?
- Is there anything else you want to say/share with the guys today?

# 3
# BROTHERHOOD

Men congregate in a variety of places for a variety of reasons. From football stadiums to backyard fire pits, from boardrooms to golf greens, we are not hard-pressed to find groupings of men engaged in all sorts of activities. The gathering of men is not an uncommon occurrence.

Recently, on a trip to visit a friend and Legacy Partner of Restoration Project, my colleague and I landed at the airport at 10 p.m. Waiting for us outside baggage claim, our host swiftly picked us up, brought us home, and started a fire outside. Though we were in Michigan in December, another friend joined us, and together we sipped whiskey, smoked cigars, and swapped stories until 1 a.m. Brutal as it was to wake up the next morning with enough clarity of mind to adequately lead the meeting we were there to facilitate, I can honestly say, the best part of the trip was the small gathering of men in the dark.

Many of us have at least some experiences similar to this. Though the depth of relationship, conversation, and connection may vary from event to event, the reality is, getting guys together is not the hard part. Men's ministries across the country have seemingly cracked the code to getting men to show up: provide bacon, smoked meat, competition, or ammunition, and guys will come out of the woodwork.

The true challenge is how to actually *connect* men. Sure, teaming up in a 4-on-4 game of basketball bonds men together against a common foe. Appealing to the primal nature of a man's stomach sits him at a table with other guys as they talk about their smokers and pick off the last bit of meat from the bone. But we all know, this is not true connection. It may be fun, but it never results in life-changing relationship.

There are five levels of masculine relationship:

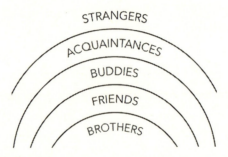

On the outermost section of the circle are all the people we have not yet met. They are **strangers**. There is nothing wrong with them. We just don't know them.

The next level inward are **acquaintances**. These are people we have met, most likely casually, and have come to recognize their faces. To move from stranger to acquaintance requires an introduction. We do not yet have a depth of relationship, but they have become men we recognize and may choose to sit next to at a conference or talk with in the narthex after church. For the most part, these are not men with whom we spend our time, but we find them to be friendly faces in a crowd of strangers. *Strangers become acquaintances through introduction.*

Sometimes, acquaintances move inward and become **buddies**. This happens through the passage of shared time when we have enough contact and interaction for us to learn we have some common interests. For example, acquaintances become buddies when we discover we share a passion for football, drive the same car, attended the same university, or play the same sport. Or we may discover similarities in our life stages, such as we each have teenage girls in the throes of puberty or soccer-playing sons. Buddies find ways to hang out together, most often with the shared interests as the centerpiece. These may be your hunting buddies, your die-hard Formula 1 guys, or even your men's small group at church. *Acquaintances become buddies through common interests.*

When I ask men, "Do you have friends?" many times they respond with, "Yes! I have a ton of guys I could call up to do something." The fact is, though our contact lists may be full of names of men we enjoy, by and large, guys live in a world primarily populated by buddies.

In order for a buddy to make the transition to **friend**, he needs to have access to your life. Friends are those people who experience life in close proximity with one another. They have made the choice to participate in each other's daily and weekly experience, and they move past their mutually shared interests into realms where they wonder, wrestle, and question together. Their time together increases, and many times their families develop connections with one another as well. These are the guys you have in your "favorites" list, as they are the men you call both in the moment of crisis (job loss or emergency) or celebration (promotion or birth of a baby). *Buddies become friends through access to your actual life.*

Recently, I conducted a small anecdotal research project. I asked a number of men (guys I don't know) how many friends they have, according to the above definition. The response was staggering. On average, they could only name *at most* two men. Two. And that was an average, meaning a large portion had none or just one. It seems most men have just a few guys they consider "friends."

It's possible that you are reading this book while part of a small group of men that is pursuing deeper and more intentional relationships with one another. For this, I commend you and count you among the very, very few who hope for such things. The path forward is mostly unpaved, as there remains one level of even deeper masculine engagement–brother.

In order for a friend to make the transition to **brother**, he needs to not only have access to your life, but also access to your *story*. Just being "life on life" with another man does not invite him into the narrowest recesses of your heart. He may know you, but until he is invited into the sacred landscape of your story, and you into his, you will not truly *know* one another. When you make the transition to brother, you commit to contend with all the false narratives that compete for your allegiance. You become witnesses to not only your current life, but also to the experience of life that brought you to the place you now are. You look down the tunnel of time into the future and link arms with Jesus on one another's behalf, to know who you are, who you have been, and who you are yet to become. *Friends become brothers through access to your story.*

> *You look down the tunnel of time into the future and link arms with Jesus on one another's behalf, to know who you are, who you have been, and who you are yet to become.*

Don't miss what I just wrote. *Your story.* Not your sin, but your story. Brothers see beyond your struggles, your failures, your challenges, and your shame, and they know who you are because they know from whence you come. They not only know *about* your struggles, they know *why those struggles are there in the first place.* Brothers read our stories and remind us who we actually are. They have become familiar with the territory of our souls and now know what it feels like to live there. It is the most intimate and connected place men know with one another.

Stranger → Acquaintance → Buddy → Friend → Brother

The most powerfully transformational masculine relationship on earth is that of a brother. Men become men through other men.[1] We grow into men through the bestowing of masculinity upon one another in the company of men. Once we become men, we need other men to "keep" us living as men. Men *stay* men through other men. Let me explain.

I have often wondered why God asks so many ridiculous questions to which He already knows the answers. In Genesis 2, He asks the first humans, Adam and Eve, after they have disobeyed and run to hide in the bushes, "Where are you?"[2] He fully knows where they are, omniscient as He is. Clearly it was not information He was seeking, but an acknowledgement from them of the rift of relationship and the loss of connection. In other words, His question is an invitation rather than a judgment.

Just a few chapters later, in Genesis 4, shortly after the fall of humanity and the exile from Eden, the world's first brothers have a contentious relationship that eventually leads to death. In Genesis 4:9, knowing Cain has murdered Abel, God asks him, "Where is your brother Abel?"

"I don't know," he [Cain] replied. "Am I my brother's keeper?"[3]

Again, God's question is not about gathering intel or interrogating suspects at a crime scene. Discovering Abel's whereabouts is not the purpose of the question. God wants Cain to grapple with what he has just done. Though we have no account of God's answer to Cain's question, "Am I my brother's keeper?" I have often wondered if God whispered under His breath, "Yes. Yes, in fact, you are."

What would it have looked like for these brothers to "keep" one another? To tend to, care for, be aware of, seek after, protect, rally for, share with, and hold each other with honor and in high regard? What we do know is the lack of such brotherly keeping resulted in the first murder in recorded history.

As you continue the journey into deeper brotherhood with one another, you will need to descend the ladder of masculine relationship one rung at a time: from strangers into acquaintances, and from acquaintances into buddies. Then move from buddies to friends, and then finally into brothers. Your group will need to become acquainted with one another, spend intentional time together, increase proximity to one another, and make some mutual commitments. For some of you, this descent is familiar, and you are among the few who can say you have a few good friends on your I.C.E.[4] list. For some of you (in fact, for many of you), this is completely uncharted territory.

But, to take the bold step into becoming brothers, you will need to learn how to keep one another's stories. In general, men are woefully unprepared to walk this path. That's okay. Let me show you the way.

## DIFFERENCE BETWEEN BROTHER AND BROTHERHOOD

There is a vast difference between the words "brother" and "brotherhood." Many of the men with whom I work have naturally born brothers, but scarce few have anyone for whom they have a deep, mutual affection and a *determination to bless*. And yet, at the core of a man's life is an intense longing to give and to receive blessing with another man, uniting them on a level superseding any sort of earthbound relationship.

### Brothers

Most often, the word "brothers" refers to a natural blood connection. It is a relationship between males merely by virtue of a familial association. This association comes without choice, having been decided for them by parents and God's design. Brothers are brothers for no other reason other than shared DNA.[5] There is no choice; It just is.

History is full of stories where biological brothers both love and feud, but mostly feud. Mythology tells the tales of several brothers who find ways to battle and undermine one another. Consider some of the more well-known myths, including Romulus and Remus; Hades, Zeus, and Poseidon; and Thor and Loki. Myths often use the brother relationship, especially twin brothers, to symbolize the dichotomy of good versus evil. The Bible is also full of feuding brothers, from Cain and Abel to Joseph and his eleven jealous brothers, from Esau and Jacob to James and John, the "Sons of Thunder" jockeying for the best seat at the heavenly table. In most of these sagas, the characters are brothers by birth and enemies by choice. The goal of one is to take the other out.

One man I know is the younger of two brothers. In their youth, as if to prove his dominance, the older brother randomly and violently attacked my friend, often beating him to the point of bloodshed. At night, he would sneak in and tear him out of bed, throwing him to the floor and poking his eyes. A deep sense of vigilance rose out of protective necessity in my friend, who later trained as a fighter. Brother set against brother.

Even when rivalry is not part of the equation, distance and absence often leave their mark on sibling relationships. Recently, I have been helping another man develop a deeper connection in his marriage. As we investigated his story, he revealed that he grew up in a home of four brothers, all of whom excelled in different areas of sports, academics, and music. This man, third in the birth order, preferred math and technology and often found himself left behind at home while the rest of the family attended sporting events, band concerts, and spelling bees. No one remembered him. No one pursued him. As a child, his need for relational attachment withered, and he simply learned to turn off his heart's longing for brotherly love. Now, as you can imagine, that has massive ramifications in his marriage. Devastation wrought when brothers turned away.[6] To this day, though they live in the same small town, he doesn't even know their phone numbers.

I have one older sister named Andrea. She was born in the late

1960s with a mental disability that incapacitated her ability to grow, thrive, or participate in "normal" activities. Even today, she cannot read, write, or communicate clearly, and there is no definition or diagnosis to identify her condition. Today, at the age of 55, she remains a mental three-year-old.

Born five years later, I quickly surpassed her in every category. As a normally developing child, I began to move, speak, and relate in ways she simply could not. Within the first year of my life, though five years younger, I soon became her "big brother." To this day, Andrea has deep, deep affection for me. To her, I am a normalizing and security-producing character in life. The reality is that I am her brother by birth although I had nothing to do with it. I had no control over my familial destiny. As we are the only two children in our family, I am bound by blood to Andrea.[7]

I distinctly remember the day I had to make my choice. We lived on a long cul-de-sac in the western suburbs of Denver, nestled against the gentle slopes of the foothills. Some of the first to purchase and build a home in this new neighborhood, we saw a dramatic increase in the number of children circling the street on their bikes, skateboards, Big Wheels, and Green Machines during our first years there.[8] One summer afternoon, as the "gang" gathered in the street, the ringleader instigated a game of keep-away, snatching the hat off my sister's head and throwing it around the circle. At that moment I knew I had to make a choice: *for* my sister or *against*. By the grace of God, I defended her. To this day, if I am proximate when she meets a new person, she is bold and intentional about introducing me as *"my brother."*[9]

Brotherhood

You see, there is something far deeper to brotherhood. Blood does not do it. It's about a choice.

In English, the suffix *–hood* indicates "participation or identification with a state or condition of being."[10] It transforms a simple noun into a community. It changes neighbors into a neighborhood, man into manhood, priest into priesthood, adult into adulthood, child into childhood, and brother into brotherhood. It increases the context to extend beyond one person with an inclination toward the communal.

Brotherhood, therefore, means more than brothers. It extends far beyond blood relationship into something participatory and communal. It means a volitional involvement in a community of men (for only men can be brothers), standing together in solidarity through the journey of life. It is a unifying of hearts toward the good and God-given purpose for each man's life. To participate in brotherhood, with blood relatives or not, is a determination to know one another's stories, to see the world through the eyes of the other, and to seek blessing and goodness for one another.

## THE BROTHERHOOD CHOICE

To participate in this Brotherhood group, you have to make a choice. You will need to step beyond yourself and open up to other men, likely in ways you have never before dared. These steps continue to be both strange and risky, and navigating these waters feels choppy and unsteady. The best relationships are usually gained by intentional risk. This is no different.

At the beginning when my brother Greg Daley and I co-founded Restoration Project, we had to step into the turbulent waters of brotherhood once again. We had been deeply committed friends for years, started a ministry together, and moved our families across the country together. Despite this, true brotherhood still takes work and intention. I had moved forward with a ministry proposal and overlooked him in the process.

I do that.

Often.

Hurt, yet determined to remain committed to one another, we wrestled our relationally capsized canoe upright and once again acknowledged our love and devotion to the good of the other. Later, Greg sent me this text: "Thx. It's good to have you as a friend. I love you." My response: "Yeah man. You too. Thanks for this morning. Let's just move to Ireland and be sheep herders." The brotherhood choice is one you make and then make again and again and again.

Some of you may have chosen to participate in this experiment with blood brothers. If this is the case, I commend you heartily. But in all likelihood, most of your group is a motley gathering of men who simply desire more from their masculine relationships. The call to something deeper, something *brotherly*, echoes in your core, and the risk of being weird or awkward with other guys has been outweighed by the potential reward.

## PERSONAL REFLECTION

- In your opinion, how would you state the difference between being a brother versus being part of a brotherhood?
- Why is it so hard for men to be in meaningful relationships with one another?
- Why is it hard for *you* to be in relationship with other men, or is it?
- How are you feeling about this process? Take note of your own feelings and hesitations. We are only in chapter three. Do you still want to do this? Are you bored? Excited? Why?
- What are you tempted to hold back or reserve with this group? What feels too dangerous?
- What do you think of the progression of Stranger -> Brother? Think about some of your closer male relationships. Where are they on that spectrum?
- Do you have a best friend? In your mind, what earns someone the title of best friend?
- What is the difference between a best friend and a brother?

## GROUP DISCUSSION

- Discuss the difference between "brother" and "brotherhood."
- Do you have a biological brother? How has that been different from "brotherhood" for you? How has it been the same?
- What do you think it takes to be part of "brotherhood"?
- Tell us about one of your more painful experiences of friendship? When was a time you were betrayed,

wounded, or abandoned by someone you considered a good friend?
- What is the history of friendship like for you? Have you ever had a best friend? Always? Rarely? Never? Do you have a man in your life now that you would call a best friend?
- What is difficult about forming deeper friendships? What scares you? What intrigues you?
- How hopeful are you for knowing and being known by a man or a group of men? How do you find yourself sabotaging that hope?
- As we continue, how can the other men in this group be aware of you? What would you like us to do, or not do, in regards to relating to you?
- What else would you like the group to know?

# 4
## SPACE

About 10 years ago, I found myself in an incredibly awkward and difficult position. As a counselor working with men, I am often invited to visit and speak in a variety of venues where men gather. One particular evening, I received an invitation from a group of men whose focal topic was addiction.

Given merely a room number amongst a church's extensive and labyrinthine halls, I should have known. Problem signpost #1. I should have stopped at the outside door and called to cancel. Knowing, however, how men (especially Christian men) have come to congregate, I pressed on, found the room, and entered. Stenciled on the walls of this small, remote classroom were cartoon animals and a giant ark.[1] White doves and bright rainbows sought to bring life and color to the room. It brought me an instant headache. Problem signpost #2.

Second to arrive, I sat down on a toddler-sized chair. My 6'3" frame curled up like a pretzel, and I introduced myself to the meeting's host. Over the next 10 minutes, only two other men joined our infantile circle. Perhaps large crowds of men originally intent on joining us either got lost in the hallways or wised up, tucked tail, and ran when they saw smiley Noah. Panic began to rise in my soul as the host made preparations to begin the meeting. Quickly, I realized there were two leaders of this group—the host and one of the other men. The fourth, a young man in his early 20s, sat silently and awkwardly about three feet back from the tiny circle. Problem signposts #3, #4, and #5.

Over the next hour, the two guests (myself and this young man) heard about the ministry's goals, origin, future, and structure. Handmade brochures circulated, and the conversational ball finally passed to the young man. Within minutes, it became painfully obvious that the young man was new and in need of help—his addiction: obsessive masturbation. Without asking him any further questions, the hosts offered a flurry of tips and strategies for the man to overcome the problem. Finally, they paused long enough to ask my opinion, giving me about 30 seconds to respond to the presenting problem of the hour. Problem signposts #6 through #29,874.

Then it was over. Handshakes and goodbyes and "thanks for coming" as we darted for the exit. It was a night of agony. It was a night of extreme disappointment. And it was a night that is likely repeated a thousand times over each evening, tucked away in the recesses of church buildings across the country.

## MAN SPACE

It doesn't take an immense amount of brilliance to know men should not be hanging out in back-corner toddler rooms. There is something categorically wrong with the scene I just described. The problem is most Christian men have experienced something painfully similar. In our attempts to go deeper with one another, we move from our smoked meat and shotgun outings into the awkward circles of plastic chairs. We trade ribs for industrial coffee and donuts and settle for stark and sterile Sunday school rooms where men find themselves anemic, pathetic, and disempowered.

Now, while not all Christian men's gatherings occur in the back-corner room, there often remains a distinct disconnection between a *man's space* and a *man's heart.*

Again, it does not take a genius. Simply consider the spaces men create for themselves. Rustic cabins with no electricity and hunting blinds in the mud. Man caves with full digitalization and surround sound. Fire pits with leaping flames and garages with concrete floors, man-chairs, lava lamps, and old Wayne Gretzky cutouts. Private studies lined with books, old leather, Scotch, and pipes. Even in metropolitan settings, severe angles, bright lights, exposed brick and beams, massive windows, and vaulted heights tend to indicate the presence of a man. There is something deeply earthy and fierce about the spaces men create.

I have recently reclaimed my basement. At various times over the last 12 years, our home's lower-level space served as my son's bedroom, a guest room, the teen hangout area, an office, an overflow TV-watching room, and a workout room. This year, my son moved out as he launched his post-graduate life, leaving the basement empty and open once again. Now, it was *my* turn to take the blank canvas and create the kind of space I wanted. My aim? A Scottish pub.

With my wife's help, we painted the walls a dark gray and then built a large bookshelf out of raw wood and industrial pipe. We gathered our books from around the house and filled the shelves completely with our decades-old collection. I bought lamps with exposed Edison bulbs and connected them to my smart home. I reoriented my oversized leather chair and ottoman, the one I bought for $30 from a thrift store years and years ago. We repurposed my father's old leather couch, as well as a glass-doored shelf that has followed us across the world, making it into my whiskey-and-liquor cabinet equipped with under-shelf remote control lighting. On the dark gray wall, we hung several framed pieces we had collected over the years, as well as the deep red upholstery curtains we had kept from our years overseas.

It was a lot of work. And it was worth it.

I finally have my man space. Now I spend hours there every morning in the darkly lit and rugged room, reading, thinking, praying, journaling. I absolutely love it. While something in my soul feels most at home in that space in my house, my hope and intent is for it to provide space for other men to join me there as well. Yes, through the years guys have gathered on my couches and around my kitchen table, but we all know, it is just not the same.

When men enter spaces such as this, something shifts. The space communicates, "You have been anticipated. You are wanted here." It invites him to open his mind, heart, and story in a way plastic chairs and Noah's ark-themed church rooms simply do not. Even everyday living rooms, while possibly comfortable and inviting, may not be designed with the heart of a man in mind.

## RED EARTH

Again, it goes back to the Garden. It usually does.

A close look at Adam's creation reveals a particularly interesting aspect to the landscape of a man's heart. In Genesis 2:7, we read, "Then the Lord God formed a man from the dust of the ground and breathed into his nostrils the breath of life, and the man became a living being."[2] From the very beginning, Adam is created from dirt. Indeed, the name "Adam" is etymologically related to the Hebrew words for ground, earth, red, and ruddy. Dust, ground, and breath are the ingredients God uses for the Adamic creation.

In the next verse, Genesis 2:8, we discover another remarkable fact: "Now the Lord God had planted a garden in the east, in Eden; and there he *put the man* he had formed."[3] It is again noted in Genesis 2:15: "The Lord God took the man and *put him* in the Garden of Eden to work it and take care of it."[4] Both of these verses give us insight as to *where* Adam was created, and it is *not* in the garden. Somewhere in the outback,[5] God creates Adam and then picks him up and places him in Eden.

There is something inherently *earthy, ruddy,* and *rustic* about

Adam. Eve, however, the pinnacle of beauty, elegance, and all creation, finds her beginning *in* the garden. While all men may not have a deep love for dirt and the outdoors,[6] I believe there is something core to a man's soul that simply cannot operate in the confines of a disinfected, sterile, or domesticated environment.

Of all the Sundays throughout the year, do you know which one has the largest degree of male truancy at church? You guessed it. Father's Day. When men are given a day in which they are honored and celebrated, and often given the choice as to how they would like to spend their day, most men opt outside. They load up their families and head to the hills, or lake, or river, or wherever they feel most connected to their masculine hearts. It is a stunning sociological reality, and one the church should wake up to if we hope to more deeply engage the men in our midst.

Several years ago at our church in Seattle, something vastly different occurred. On Father's Day, our pastor called the men to show up to the field behind the church early and to bring a picture of their family. He made sure that every family in the church was represented by a man, especially those families without husbands or fathers. Outside, surrounded by underbrush and trees, men gathered under a large tent around a massive wooden table set with flickering flames from countless candles. As we entered the tent, we took off our shoes and walked on the bare earth. No music, no confines, and no pretense. One by one, each man prayed aloud for the members of his family and set the picture on the table. And one by one, men began to weep. Together.

The difference, I believe, between the Father's Day inside the building and the Father's Day in the earth-bound tent is the intentionality of creating a space *for men*, where men can let down their defenses, enter in, and connect with the Edenic dirt of their souls.

## SANCTIFICATION OF TIME, HUMANITY, AND SPACE

To sanctify means "to set apart and make holy." It transforms the normal and familiar into something meaningful. In the scriptures, we see the interaction of the Eternal God with the finite creation in the sanctification of three elements: time, humanity, and space.

In the Genesis account, God creates the heavens and the earth. In six days, He makes everything and seems to have a raucously good time. At the end of each day, He sits back in joy, throws His hands in the air, and calls His work "good!" It is as if the Master Artist, covered from head to toe in smears of paint, sits back to view the glory of His work and cries "Yes!" After completing all of creation in the first six days, He sets apart a whole day to do nothing but bask in His fullness of joy. The seventh day He makes holy, and later He reminds humanity, or rather *commands* humanity, to do the same.[7] From the first days of creation, a certain amount of time is to be sanctified and set apart.

Similarly, from the beginning God set apart one of His creatures as special, holy, and uniquely representative of Himself. As image bearers of God, humanity alone received the blessing of sanctification. Indeed, sinfulness and fallenness have marred our holy standing, yet it is Christ's incarnational purpose to restore us all to our rightful place as heirs and children of the King. In both Leviticus and 1 Peter,[8] God is clear to call us to holiness because of His holiness. After the sanctification of time, humanity is sanctified. God is the singular actor in both of these actions. He set aside the Sabbath, and He set aside humanity. We had nothing to do with it.

But space is an entirely different thing.

God gave space to humanity. In Genesis 1:28, He says, "Be fruitful and increase in number, fill the earth and subdue it."[9] Subdue it. Rule over it. Fill it. Work it. It's *yours*. And in some way, create places to meet with one another and with the Divine.[10] Indeed, "[t]he God who made the world and everything in it is the Lord of heaven and earth and does not live in temples built by human hands."[11] God doesn't need sanctified space. We do. We are the ones who need to separate the common from the Divine. We are the ones who need to remember[12] our story, our place, our future, and our God. We are the ones who should "not give up meeting together."[13]

As a result, He has given us the ability to create spaces that invoke in our own souls different feelings, perspectives, and responses. Architecture, therefore, is both the mastery of physics and geometry, as well as the invitation of spacial emotion. Consider the message of the architect who designs a Gothic cathedral versus one who designs the post office. Or how Google utilizes space[14] in their offices to inspire creativity and playfulness versus how courtrooms architecturally establish a power differential between judge and defendant.

When it comes to the Divine, God partners with humanity to sanctify space. In his book, *Given*, poet Wendell Berry tells us, "There are no unsacred places; there are only sacred places and desecrated places."[15] Throughout the scriptures, "holy ground" is found when people and God meet. At times, altars are established or structures are built. At other times, four cloth walls create a roving tabernacle in which God's presence is said to rest. The sanctification of space, therefore, is created by men in collaboration with God. Yet among men, and especially with Christian men's gatherings, we deny the power of intentionally sacred space by anesthetizing it, domesticating it, or paying it no attention at all. The ease of creating sacred space can be among the simplest aspects of men's gatherings, yet more often than not, it sinks to the end of the priority list below the folding chairs and sausage links.

As I attend to masculine space in my counseling room, for example, I have taken what was a sterile dentist's office and transformed it into a place of masculine comfort and rest. Leather couches, rusted metal items from the vintage store, dark wood flooring, and earth tone walls subtly tell men they have been anticipated. A shelf with books, a photograph of men around a bonfire, and metal artwork adorn the walls. I have specifically chosen each element to create a space that communicates, "You can rest your manhood here."

There is an old Chassidic story about a boy in the woods. Every afternoon he disappears into the wild, and no one seems to know where he goes or what he does. One day, his father follows him, only to find him talking with the trees and communing with the animals. When asked why he escapes to the forest every day, the boy replies, "I go to be with God." Hoping to reassure him, his father reminds him of God's omnipresence, that He is the same everywhere. The boy wisely responds, "I know, but I am not."[16]

You see, space matters.

In the end, I believe attentiveness to space helps men dive below the surface more quickly, more easily, and with more trust than if they were to find themselves pretzeled in a toddler chair. While man space does not guarantee anything, it makes deeper connection between men far more likely.

## CREATING BROTHER SPACE

If men are to engage one another in ways that are meaningful and purposeful, we need to create the appropriate spaces that will *disarm masculine defenses*, allow us to *initiate masculine conversations*, and encourage us to *uphold masculine confidences*.

### Disarming Masculine Defenses

When I walked into that "Noah's ark" church classroom, I immediately felt my defenses go on high alert. The possibility of masculine engagement instantly shut down the moment I entered the room.

A common misnomer in men's groups is that men need icebreakers and simple activities to get conversations rolling. While this has an element of truth, it is a pea-sized attempt to overcome monolithic defenses, often resulting in pseudo-sharing and pseudo-connection that lasts for a few minutes until the bell rings and the round is over. Rarely do these conversations carry over into long-term friendships. A good rule of thumb: if the activity has a point or a message, it's doomed to avoid relationship and provides only a point or a message. Men inevitably get missed.

At one men's breakfast I attended, the speaker had us wad up pieces of paper and then throw them blindfolded into a trash can as other men coached us. The point was for us to learn to rely on one another in our faith journey. In essence, we can sometimes make a basket alone, but we have a far better chance when we work together. Indeed, a good concept, and as you can see, I remember the activity. The real question is, do I remember the *men?* The answer is no. The activity became the point, not the men. I have absolutely no recollection of them. Was the activity a success in making a point? Yes. But it did nothing to facilitate the real change found in the connected and intimate relationships between men.

In order to disarm masculine defenses, I have found men need *experiential spaces*. Rather than focusing on conversation, content, or the message as the primary purpose of the engagement, men need experiences that are in and of themselves engaging. It is the shared experience that is the point. It is not the experience of the what, but the experience of the who.

*It is not the experience of the what, but the experience of the who.*

Several years ago, I had the distinct privilege of gathering men from various seasons of my life. These men had shared in my journey on a variety of levels. Some of them I had known for almost 20 years; others I had just met. In December, men from across the country descended on a small ranch in Wyoming. While they all knew me, few of them knew each other.

Over the three days we spent together, we had few rules and lots of experiences. We had snowmobiles, shotguns and skeet shooting, ax throwing, ATVs, and board games. Each man chose his experience. I personally stayed away from the guns, but I found a way to flip a snowmobile. Others blasted clay pigeons from the sky, while still others warmed their feet by the fire with a 16-year-old Scotch. Though the overall purpose of our gathering was to connect on deeper levels as men, we allowed the organic connections to occur over time without manufacturing them or forcing them into an agenda.

For an experiential space to be meaningful to men, four elements seem to be essential. It must be undomesticated, risky, together, and men only.

**Undomesticated** Just as a boy will try to climb to the highest branch on a tree or swim to the deepest part of the pool, men also need space to stretch the limits. Domesticity needs to take a back seat, and rules and regulations must be exchanged for freedom, wildness, and ruggedness. The boundaries between man and nature need to be removed in order to facilitate connection between men. As a simple example, the owner of this Wyoming ranch grew concerned about the number of people using the toilet, fearing it would overload his septic tank over the course of the weekend. Even though temperatures in Wyoming in December are often subzero, he asked the men to take their urinary needs outside. Within a few hours, the snow around the back of his home grew various shades of yellow. Most domesticated contexts require the use of a toilet, yet simply asking men to pee outside somehow added to the rugged nature of our gathering. It created an atmosphere of freedom that translated into a sense of "all being men, together."[17]

Men's retreats attempt to do this by heading to a somewhat remote outdoor location. Log buildings, rugged fireplaces, and hearty food provide a tremendous start. Unfortunately, autocratic groundskeepers often govern the camp facilities, and safety nets and corporate insurance regulations keep men from stretching the limits.[18]

As a native of Colorado, I recognize I have a certain bent to my thinking. Even today, as I work on this manuscript, I took my laptop, chair, and water bottle to the forest in order to enter the headspace to write. Many men, however, do not have as intense a drive for wild natural spaces. In fact, some men fear, avoid, or find it distasteful. In no way am I attempting to say that all men must be outdoorsmen if they are to truly be men. I am saying, however, that something seems to happen for a large number of men when we remove the bounds of civilization and introduce them once again to "rules-free living." For some, this means mountains. For others, it means the beach. For some, it means a finely aged Scotch. For others, it is an engagement with the beauty of opera. Whatever it means for you, my hope is that it translates into one word: *freedom*. Freedom to risk being who and how God made you without limits, judgment, or fear.

**Risk** Several years ago, I took my wife snowmobiling. The two of us loaded onto a machine and took to the hills. We witnessed high vistas and quiet forests, pristine in their snow-covered beauty. I drove the snowmobile with care, making sure not to bank too swiftly or exceed "safe" speeds. I treated my precious cargo with care.

At this December men's gathering, however, another man and I lined up our two snowmobiles in a field parallel to I-80. Simultaneously, we launched out at full throttle, racing the semi-trucks on the highway, approaching speeds of 70 mph. Bouncing along the frozen tundra, I felt the roar of the motor match the pace of my heart. Later, riding tandem with another man, we banked the snowmobile too high and rolled the machine. It was glorious.

To some degree, risk must be part of men's experience. While I would have never taken my wife on such a risky joyride, there was no question I would push the limits with my friend. Risk does not mean recklessness, but rather an experience of speed or heights or explosives or sharp objects beyond what is typically acceptable. It is part of a boy's rite of passage to do dangerous things in the company of other men. Providing opportunities to stretch the limits creates a sense of unity in the group.

Risk for some men may have nothing to do with adrenaline. Risk for some might mean showing up in the company of other men at all. For many guys, men have been a significant source of disappointment, pain, or abuse. Ridicule, separation, abandonment, or feelings of difference have kept men from entering places where other men exist. Some men have found a safe harbor among women. Risk, therefore, simply means entering the room because rooms of men have repetitively proven dangerous.

**Together** Now, any man could hop on an ATV or load up a shotgun alone, and many do. But there is something deeply important about doing these things *with* other men. To race the semis would have been thrilling regardless, but to see the face of my friend as it reddened with the bitter Wyoming wind and to high-five him upon our return to the warmth of the fire was absolutely priceless. Creating history together with another man will inevitably lower defenses and provide an opportunity for deeper engagement later.

Among the greatest maladies of mankind today, loneliness and isolation sit at the peak. We have found ways to distance ourselves from true relationship. Even extroverts express a deep sense of aloneness despite often being in the presence of others. Togetherness begins with proximity, but it must penetrate further into aspects of the real heart and grit of life. Even when words are not spoken, the mere presence of another man has the potential to transform the experience to one of meaningful history.

**Men Only** This should go without saying. A palpable atmospheric shift occurs when men withdraw from the feminine. Highly defended against one another, men also have extremely well-crafted walls and façades in place in the presence of women. It is vital for men to regularly create spaces where they are just men. In mixed company, men are often far more concerned about what others will think. They worry about disappointing their wives or being seen as weak or vulnerable. But when men are allowed to retreat from the world of responsibility for others and settle into a space where they are only responsible for themselves, an inner sense of calm, reflection, and ease can exist. Men need to be physically transported to a new place, away from family, technology, and duty in order to find the way to their hearts.

Unfortunately, "men only" has come to have a variety of negative meanings. First, our society interprets this often as a misogynistic exclusion of women. Indeed, men in the past have taken this too far, having men-only clubs and lounges that demean the inherent value of women. In addition, a "gentlemen's club" is a cowardly place for men to pervertedly objectify women.[19] In no way do I condone "men only" spaces for such practices or purposes.

The purpose for men only in this context has nothing to do with women and far more to do with men. Men who withdraw from the world of women often have their wits about them and find themselves more free to access parts of their masculine hearts that normally remain under lock and key.

## INITIATE MASCULINE CONVERSATIONS

Shifting from the external factors that disarm masculine defenses and create experiential spaces, we now turn toward the internal experiences of a man's heart. While "manly" experiences may be interpreted as events (such as the shooting and ATV riding described above), true masculine experiences emerge from a context of honest conversation.

You have likely heard (and experienced) men typically talk far less than women. While this stereotype may hold an inkling of truth, the reality is that men need to talk just as much. We need to share our experiences and process our thoughts. We need to hear the stories of others in order to make sense of our own. Therefore, some of the most deeply masculine times are when men enter into honest conversation with one another. Often, the most memorable times of men-only camping trips are the hours around the fire, where men tell their tales, open their lives, and hear the experiences of others.

Consider the delight of having a group of trusted men listen to your stories of growth, challenge, failure, and despair. Imagine the elation of knowing that the landscape of your heart is known, validated, and affirmed by other men. Think about the relief you might experience just in knowing that your brother has your back—or that he even knows what that means to you. Men have such ambivalence toward letting others know the landscape of their souls. We want it, and we are so deeply terrified of it. All of us are desperate to be found, yet we do everything we can to remain hidden because we fear being found out.

Masculine conversations are those that mutually pursue, wrestle, define, confirm, sharpen, wrangle, correct, and enjoy the heart of another man. This can only occur when the defenses are down, history is built, trust is established, and brotherhood is created.[20] Somehow this is both an organic and an intentional place. It does not just happen, yet it cannot be forced. When it comes to our lives and our stories, there can be no breaking and entering. We must prepare for and then await the invitation, and then we walk into the landscape of another man's story with reverence, awe, and a recognition we have now entered a sacred place.

Uphold Masculine Confidences

While the term "holding confidence" may be generally understood as "keeping secrets," it is my hope to modify this understanding to include far more. Indeed, vital to true and honest conversation between men is the notion of confidentiality. However, both society and the church have lost the deeper meaning of what it means to uphold another's confidence.

The word "confidence" has two primary roots. First, the prefix *con-* means "together" or "with." We find this throughout the English language. *Con*gruent. *Con*tinue. *Con*struct. *Con*gregation. *Con*firm. In each of these cases (and far too many others to list here), *con-* identifies an element of connectedness, where the *withness* of God is found. Emmanuel, meaning "God *with* us," descended from heaven and took on mortal flesh through the incarnation of Jesus. In a cosmic shift, the Most High became human in order to come alongside our lost race. In the same way, a man who comes alongside another, though momentarily and possibly poorly, reflects the *with-*

*ness* of God in his solidarity with his brother. To be *with* has immense implications. At the core, men long for other men to be with them in the experience of what it means to exist. No judgment. No fixing. No advice. Just to know and be known.

Often, as I work with men in my counseling office, I intentionally focus the first few sessions on coming alongside them in their experience, their pain, their confusion, and their story. While I may ask questions, my focus is on inviting a conversation that allows the man to just be himself. As an example, one time a man who entered my office sensed the freedom to let down his guard, and he wept for most of the hour. All I said was, "It's okay for you to just be you."

Secondly, confidence's primary root is *fide,* meaning "faith." Most popularly known in the doctrinal term *"sola fide,"* which means "by faith alone" from the Protestant Reformation, the term refers to a belief and hope in its object.

Belief and hope and faith.

In the internal world of a man's heart, therefore, upholding confidence equates to a brotherly commitment to hold faith with one another. It is a genuine removal of masculine isolation by fostering a solidarity that grows exponentially in the brotherhood of men. It says, "I have faith *with* you and *in* you because I have seen and known your heart."

What would it be like to look another man in the eye and hear him boldly say those words…to you? It is what most men long for, yet they are the most unlikely words ever spoken. Creating space for men to hold faith with one another sets the stage for such things to be said.

It is no surprise, then, that weak coffee, stale donuts, and inane activities in white-washed classrooms will never, ever create the space for men to truly engage one another. I cringe at the thought and long for so much more.

## PERSONAL REFLECTION

- What have been your most tragic men's group experiences? *Where* have they happened?
- Think about how you are wired. What kinds of spaces do you create for yourself? (Or what does or what would your ideal man cave look like? Wilderness? Luxury? Dirt and mud, or books and leather?)
- Consider some of your most significant experiences with men (not necessarily in a formal men's group setting). Where did those occur?
- As you think of the categories of Undomesticated, Risk, Together, and Men Only, which one feels most familiar? Which is most unknown to you?
- What happens to your heart when you enter a space for men that feels overly domesticated?
- Many men do not consider their environment as an important aspect of their inner lives. What moves do you want to make in your space to create an experiential space for men? What would that take?
- As you think about gathering with the other guys this week, what do you think their thoughts and responses will be to this section?
- How does space impact your relationship with God? Does it? What changes do you need to make for yourself personally in order to better connect with Him spiritually?
- As you consider the Brotherhood gathering, are there any changes you would want to make in your Brotherhood space?

## GROUP DISCUSSION

*Today take some time to observe your space. Where are you gathered? What do you notice? What, if anything, has occurred to make this a masculine space? What still needs to happen? If you find yourselves in a sterile, domesticated place, find a better place...now. Talk about it, and then go there before continuing your gathering.*

- Tell some stories about your past experiences with bad man spaces.
- Talk about the concepts of Undomesticated, Risk, Together, and Men Only. Do you agree or disagree? Do you connect with those?
- Consider the word *confidence*. What are your thoughts with regard to *con* and *fide*?

*Note: I want you to see that I am pushing your group to talk about talking. We just don't do that as much as men, but it is necessary for you to create the space now in order for the upcoming weeks to be more meaningful.*

- What connotation does "men only" have in your mind?
- What experiences of "men only" have you had, good or bad? Do you hesitate to be with only men?
- Consider the concept of Adam being called "red earth." What do you think God intended?
- What needs to be done differently in the upcoming weeks for you to experience more openness in this Brotherhood group?
- Is there anything else you would like to say/share with the guys today?

# 5
# WHAT IS YOUR STORY? PART I

I grew up in Colorado and had been gone for over 20 years. Just over a decade ago, the call of the Rockies got the best of me. After living in Chicago, Michigan, the Middle East, and Seattle, the echoes of my Rocky Mountain upbringing could no longer be silenced. I *had* to move back to *my mountains*. Although I lived both highs and lows in each of those places, my heart belongs where blue skies, low humidity, mountain streams, and pine trees call home.

With the help of a few good men, I packed a massive U-Haul with an overwhelming load of our junk, and it strained as I aimed it from Seattle to my birthplace of Colorado. All at once, I felt the exhilaration of a few days on the road and the anticipation of new movement in my heart. Though a man approaching middle age, at that moment I was both an adult and a child.

An adult because I faced a new and unknown future.

A child because my father was riding shotgun.

After a day of intense packing, during which the children's swing set was dismantled and hoisted over the roof of our little rambler as a donation to a friend, I climbed into the cab of the U-Haul and noticed something utterly terrifying. There was no sound system of any kind. No Bluetooth, no CD player, no old-school cassette tape player. Not even a radio. Nothing to shield my father and me from the scream of silence. My plans for music, podcasts, playlists, books-on-tape, or even talk radio for our journey instantly disintegrated. The starkness of the upcoming 1,273 miles came into full focus. We were destined for three days of unconversational conversation.

While my father and I have a cordial relationship, neither of us would consider it full of communication. We typically talk about "stuff," but not really about the real stuff of life. For the first few hours, we talked around simple topics, such as "So, how's your car working?" and "Do you have people to help unload?" Every 50 miles or so, we'd circle back around to similar questions without any hope of escape from the conversational vortex that bound us. We had two old-school GPS units and set them to duel on the dashboard, one speaking as a British female and the other as an American male. Both insistent, both rude. At least they had something new to say every few miles.

Somewhere in Idaho's open-road vastness, the pounding in my soul grew unbearable, and I knew I could not survive another rotation around the conversational drain. The present reality of our small U-Haul universe and the unchanging bleakness of the road offered no hope for deeper connection. Conversations about the future had been repetitively chewed, with all questions and possibilities thoroughly explored over and over again. The only remaining option was a return to the past...a return to story. It was our only escape.

With one simple question, I altered the atmosphere in that stark cab, and the remaining miles seemed to churn more quickly than before. "Dad," I asked, "what was it like for you when I was growing up? I have memories, but I don't know the bigger story."

## METANARRATIVE

In that moment, with that uncomplicated inquiry into his story, I entered a narrative larger than myself. I exited the confines of the truck and began to explore a reality I lived through but never fully knew. As my father began to talk, he shared stories of the world in which I existed, though I lacked any concept of the greater forces at work around me. I was born into an already-existing story, the trajectory of which deeply affected my life, yet like a cruise ship at sea, I had no idea I was even in motion. My world, my perspectives, my experiences, and my memories existed only as a singular perspective of a complicated universe that involved forces far beyond my comprehension or awareness. As a child, my life was a subplot to his story.

He told me about the time his law firm almost closed because of the lack of work.

He told me how his parents dropped him off at law school in the 1960s with a vintage trunk of clothes, a $20 bill, a handshake and pat on the shoulder followed by a brief, "Good luck."

He told me how he had to step in and create state- and county-wide social services for developmentally disabled children because none existed for my mentally and physically disabled sister.

He told me about his near midlife crisis that would have catapulted him (and us) from a metropolitan attorney to a high-country hay rancher.

He told me how it had been for him to send me to Germany as an exchange student at the age of 16. It so happened to be 1989, the year the Berlin Wall fell and the communist block plummeted into chaos, sending Eastern Europe into a grand upheaval. His son was in the middle of it, and it scared him.

He told me what it was like to have my grandmother, his mother-in-law, live with us for years.

He told me stories, and he gave me the bigger picture. He pulled back the curtain on the metanarrative of my life. And in that confined U-Haul cab, those miles on the open road turned into relived moments. I may have had the information about those events in his life, but I never knew what it felt like to live them. I came to understand my own life experiences as I understood more about his.

Each of us is born into a larger story. The train is already in motion, and we find ourselves flung into the already existing trajectory of human history. Everything we live is in the context of story, for there is a greater narrative that tells a much larger story. As we reshape our understanding of the itinerary of our lives, transforming our memories from a mere series of events into themes and patterns and purpose and meaning, we discover a much grander narrative than we ever imagined. As men become men through other men, it is in the sharing of our stories that we discover the depth of our own souls. As Daniel Taylor writes, "Stories make it possible for us to be human."[1] For each of us, it is our underlying story that longs to be told because stories are what connect us to one another.

We are all stories. Every one of us.

## METANARRATIVE OF GOD

Our lives are story because God is a storyteller. From the very beginning, He sought to reveal Himself to us through the telling of stories. There is not one moment or aspect or scene or movement of God in the Bible that is not surrounded by purposeful narrative. Regardless of the biblical literary genre, story informs its telling. The Psalms deepen in meaning when we understand their context. The Epistles brighten and become more human when their background is revealed. The Old Testament is written and experienced in the greater narrative of the ancient Near East, and apocalyptic scripture is best understood through the lens of the greater context of God's intention from the very beginning of time. Ancient men and women of faith come alive when we comprehend the world in which they lived. God loves stories, for it is in stories we find our meaning.[2]

What are Moses and the Exodus without the context and history of slavery? Who is Hagar without Sarai? What purpose exists for a life-saving ark without the people's befuddlement with regard to rain? Who is David without Goliath or Saul? What role does young Timothy have without his apprenticeship to Paul? What does Jesus's

Last Supper mean without the ancient celebration of Passover? God is the great Storyteller because stories tell us where we are in the greater narrative of His story. The more we understand the larger story, the metanarrative of God, the more we come to know ourselves. We are participants in His story. Just as I gained clarity for my own life experiences by understanding more about the context of my father's story, so, too, we come to know ourselves more as we increasingly orient our hearts and minds to the story of God.

Stories inform us. They shape us and give us place. They tell us who and how and why we exist. As Dan Allender says,

> Our own life is the thing that most influences and shapes our outlook, our tendencies, our choices and our decisions. It is the force that orients us toward the future, and yet we don't give it a second thought, much less a careful examination. It's time to listen to our own story.[3]

As men especially, we shy away from investigating or sharing our stories because we like to hover at the level of itinerary and disengagement. If Allender is correct (and I believe he is), then what keeps us from thinking about, examining, and listening to our stories? As John O'Donohue explains, "Your identity is not equivalent to your biography."[4] Your general demographics do not actually tell us who you are. Your story is far more than the facts. Your story is your experience, what those facts felt like, and how they shaped the man you are today.

For many men, to tell someone else their story is tantamount to heart-level exposure that feels raw, naked, and risky. Yet the more we become fluent in our stories, the more we settle into our own skin and recognize the greater purpose to our lives. In turn, hearing the stories of other men opens us up to greater possibilities and allows us to orient ourselves in God's metanarrative.

## ANATOMY OF STORY

Every good story has four primary parts. This is because the primary structure of story is eternally written by the Author and can be found clearly in the narrative of scripture.[5] Story begins with innocence, moves too quickly into tragedy, spends most of its time and focus on the struggle, and ultimately seeks restoration.

Innocence

In the beginning are scenes of innocence, where there is joy and beauty and *shalom*.[6] This is the Edenic[7] origin of earthly existence. Here, all is good. This is Genesis 1 and 2, where peace, laughter, fun, and play create the context and purpose of life. Intimacy with one another and with God mark the time of innocence. There exists no strife, no pain, no disappointment, and no worry. Deep connection forms the bedrock of all life and relationships.

Imagine the opening scenes of most movies or novels. The first few minutes set the stage for goodness and peace: whether it involves scenes of a couple in a Parisian café with lattes and croissants or of the lush serenity of the Shire; whether an older couple strolls slowly yet happily down the street or a child walks in a field of grain humming a tune. Innocence is where the story begins.[8]

Innocence here has two meanings: not guilty and naïve. Thus far in most narratives, goodness reigns and the opportunity for wrongdoing has yet to arrive. The characters in the innocent portion of the plot remain, by and large, not guilty. They enjoy the blissful experience of shalom.

Additionally, innocence also means they are naïve. They are unaware of what lies ahead and of the choices they will have to make. They have no suspicion or fear of the presence of evil or the destruction it will bring. The characters are ignorant of the formidable onslaught against them that lies just around the corner.

In most men's lives, innocence is found in boyhood. It is where he climbs trees, digs up bugs, jumps his bike on homemade ramps, and lies on the trampoline looking at the stars. It is long summer days at the pool and the soft sweetness of Mom's gentle songs. And while the boy struggles with both his own fallenness, such as his temptation to lie about completing his chores or stealing an extra cookie from the pantry, and the fallenness of the world around him as he encounters the pain of scraped knees or broken toys, he remains mostly not guilty and wonderfully naïve to the immensity of evil. He just doesn't know. Yet.

For some boys, this time of innocence is wonderfully long, lasting many years into adolescence. He is shielded from the effects of evil and lives freely without an awareness of darkness. But for many, many others, memories of true shalom are painfully short or altogether nonexistent, prematurely cut off by pain, abuse, loss, or confusion. The window of innocence is far too short, and we are abruptly catapulted out of innocence into an awareness we wished we never knew.

By God's original design, we were each intended to live eternally in innocence. Let that sink in for a moment. We were *designed* for innocence. God's purpose for humanity involved living contentedly forever with Him in Eden. Innocence, or rather, naivety to evil and a not-guilty life, was His intent for all of us all along. He made us for Eden.

But for all of us, because of our fallen ancestry, innocence inevitably ends. In the biblical narrative, it only lasts for two chapters. The window of innocence is painfully short.

## Tragedy

Too quickly, Genesis 3 shatters the peace and innocence of Eden. The Fall of humanity tragically obliterates the supreme goodness of God's creation and sends it into a downward and unrecoverable tailspin. Tragedy enters the scene and sends us all careening off course.

At the moment Adam and Eve mistrust God's good provision,

they face the marring disconnection from intimacy by evil. Tragically and traumatically, they lose innocence and face a world of pain God never intended for them to know. Evil shatters their shalom[9] and forces them to leave the protected confines of innocence.

Many children face evil at a premature age, forced to reconcile their childlike innocence with the overwhelming forces of darkness they encounter. The abandonment of a father. The predatory trap of an abuser. The withholding of love, attention, or affection from a mother. The dark, scary hallways at night while parents party till dawn. The death of a parent, which forces a child to become an adult too early. Exposure to pornography at a sleepover. The "weird" moments with a Scoutmaster.

There comes a moment in every boy's life when his innocence is wrenched away and he becomes acutely aware of evil and pain. The veil of naivety is lifted, and he begins to see the horror of his non-Edenic reality. He experiences the blunt-force trauma of a fractured world, and he must grapple with his loss of innocence as he must now find ways to survive. This is more than a scraped knee or a lost ball. It is the heart-dislocating destruction of his shalom.

For some, this tragedy has a capital "T." These are seismic moments shattering any hope of innocence. These are the scenes of abuse or loss—when his arm is broken by a drunken father; when his mother dies of cancer; when his neighbor sexually abuses him; when he witnesses his sister's suicide. We readily recognize these as tragedies and are aware of their horrific impact on a life. Like a raging gorilla with a sword, capital "T" tragedies hack deep scars into the soul.

Now, I have spoken with countless men who tell me, "But I don't have those kinds of trauma or tragedy in my past. I was never abused, my parents are still lovingly together, and I can honestly say I had a great childhood!" For those who can claim such things, I am sincerely grateful. To have known goodness such as this is truly a gift. Yet we have an enemy determined to steal, kill, and destroy all who resemble the Father. To have escaped the overt assault of capital

"T" tragedy does not indicate the complete absence of harm. Indeed, though a parent may do everything in his or her power to provide safety, security, and deep connection with a child, no one lives in Eden. No one. Despite our best efforts, there is no safe and perfect place any longer. As a result, rather than an overt attack, for some, tragedy shows up far more covertly.

Many men deflect the reality of trauma in their lives because, they reason, others have had it far worse. To name smaller harm feels lesser and unmanly, and men are conditioned to "push through the pain" as if it was of no consequence. To "man up" has come to mean to deny the power of trauma. Yet tragedy with a little "t" has the same shalom-shattering effect. The absence of a father's love, the shaming words of a coach, early exposure to pornography, and the mocking ridicule of the bully all have a tragic impact. Whereas capital "T" tragedy involves death by sword, tragedy with a little "t" looks far more like death by a thousand paper cuts. We all have lost our innocence merely by existing in a tragic world.

One general way I like to think about "T" and "t" tragedy is this: capital "T" tragedies generally result from something that *happens*, whereas small "t" tragedies result from something that *does not happen*. For example, the experience of a violent father's outburst, with the screaming, shoving, and resulting bloody nose cause a "T" trauma. It happened. Similarly impactful, yet far less likely to be considered a trauma, a "t" tragedy occurs when the boy comes home from school every day to an empty house and nothing but a TV dinner to eat. The "t" tragedy is in the absence of the emotional and relational connection he needs.

Both "T" and "t" tragedies shatter shalom. In order to truly read our stories, we must be willing to name both.

Struggle

The bulk of human existence is a struggle. We battle tragedy and groan with our loss of innocence. Tragedy has irrevocably changed the very fabric of our lives, and we wrestle with the reality of our broken world. We know deep inside that life was not meant to be this way, but we are stuck in the battle with seemingly no way out. This is Genesis 3:5 all the way through Revelation 21. In the beginning we are banished from the tree of life only to draw close to it once again at the end.[10] In between, we struggle.

Our tragedies, both "T" and "t," create for us thematic overtures with which we wrestle most of our lives. Our addictions, our successes, our interests, our relationships, and our faith all bear the marks of our struggle to overcome our tragedies. We contend with the reality that we are fallen creatures living in a fallen world. Every vacation, every video game or social media scrolling, every movie, every one-too-many-drinks, every plan for retirement, and every exhausted flop on the couch represents our deep desire to escape the struggle and to dissociate from our lives in order to return to shalom.

As innocent young boys when tragedy strikes, we grapple with the confusing reality of life's brokenness and disconnection. Somehow we *know* this is not how it is supposed to be, yet we are faced with the stark reality of how hard and painful it is. So, with all the wisdom and experience our little boys can muster, we develop ways of surviving. Like our first parents, we run to the bushes to hide our loss of innocence, we sew ever-bigger fig leaves, and we develop complex defenses to protect our now lonely hearts. We turn toward addiction, money, prestige, power, escape, shame, anger, or even hyper-spirituality to cover our vulnerability, and we do everything we can to deflect others from seeing our nakedness. We are desperate to be found but terrified to be seen.

*We are desperate to be found but terrified to be seen.*

As a therapist, I am convinced that most of our relational, emotional, and mental health struggles are deeply connected with our attempts to navigate and contend with our loss of innocence. The world is broken, and so are we, and we do everything we can to survive the shipwreck.

Restoration

And then, at the end of all things in every good story, evil is vanquished and true life is restored: Sauron topples, Voldemort is defeated, the White Witch is smashed, Commodus falls, Hitler commits suicide, and the bully gets what's coming to him. Why? Because at the end of the biblical narrative, death is destroyed and God's story ends with full and complete restoration. His original purposes are brought full circle, and Revelation 21 and 22 culminate in a triumphal renewal of the earth and humanity as He originally intended us to be. Innocence and Eden are fully restored.

The fact is, true and final restoration does not come for us here on this earth. The dénouement[11] of our story comes once and for all at God's finishing of all things. He restores, remakes, and renews. Nowhere in the scriptures does God obliterate the earth and start over completely. Instead, he returns all creation to its glorious beginnings. He does not destroy us. He restores us. He does not make new things. He makes all things new...again.[12]

That is His story. That is my story. That is your story. Do you know it? Do you tell it?

| STORY ELEMENT | GOD'S NARRATIVE | HUMAN NARRATIVE | BIBLICAL STRUCTURE |
|---|---|---|---|
| Innocence | Eden (Shalom) | Childhood Innocence | Genesis 1-2 |
| Tragedy | Fall | Shattered Shalom | Genesis 3 |
| Struggle | Life | Wrestling with Tragedy | Genesis 3:5- Revelation 20 |
| Restoration | Renewal | Christ's Return | Revelation 21-22 |

Men often deny the power of their stories and settle for a smaller narrative that feels more comfortable. To look at the whole of one's life requires tremendous honesty and reflection. It mandates the naming of the story elements of innocence, tragedy, struggle, and the hope of restoration. Sometimes, it's just too hard, especially with other men.

And so we turn on the game, grab a beer, and try to forget that we were made for something epic. Unfortunately, many men's ministries unknowingly collude with this escape and seek to change lives through the offering of more content and information. Do this. Don't do that. Consider this. Become that. Think about this. Practice that. If you just understood x, y, z, then you could change your life and become the man you want to be. The fact is, no one is changed by information. True transformation comes when our stories are both told and carefully engaged by others. Change and healing happen in the space of relationship.

## CONTENT AND CONTEXT

People vigilantly defend their pasts even though they know it is the past that binds them to destructive patterns in the present. We belittle the effects of our stories, for we believe that to be affected means we have not contended well. Shame turns inward, and we self-protect.

I recently sat with Samuel, a young man who told me his tale of an extremely abusive past. At the age of 2, his biological father left him with a poverty-stricken mother. Within months, she was pregnant again and soon married another violent man. Shortly after the birth of Samuel's half-brother, this man also left. Hungry for love and protection, his mother remarried yet again, this time to a man whose violence spilled out like poison.

At age 7, Samuel was sexually abused by a neighbor. At age 9, Samuel lived in a different home in a different state, yet it happened again. At the age of 10, Samuel was often left alone to care for his two younger half-brothers, feeding them, bathing them, entertaining them, protecting them, wondering when and if his parents would ever return from their late-night wanderings. In drunken rages, their "father" beat them. Throughout Samuel's childhood, he never knew peace. Vigilance made a much better ally.

Finally, at the age of 17, after witnessing a violent beating of his younger brother, Samuel had enough and chased the vicious man down the street with a baseball bat. Now, at the age of 30, Samuel is coming to counseling because of high levels of anxiety, night terrors, alcoholism, and an inability to develop deep, long-lasting, non-chaotic relationships.

In a matter of about 10 minutes, he laid out this tragic tale as if he were reading from a script. Listening to his words, I noticed it was as though he was recounting the hits, runs, and outs of a baseball game. He spoke matter-of-factly and looked at me with solemnity and distance. This was the content of his story.

Content is the *what*, and it is important. It is the timeline of events that lays out the overall picture of the story, yet it is usually where most man-to-man conversations end. Hovering over difficult topics somewhere close to a 30,000-foot cruising altitude, men will often acknowledge the topographical difficulties in their stories with barely a grimace. For the most part, men share the events of their lives without an emotional connection to the experience. Men may share what happened, but they keep a safe distance from talking about what it actually felt like. While it is important to know the content of one's stories, it is far more insightful to have an eye and ear to the context.

Context is *how* it felt to live the story. It is the surrounding details and the emotion with which the content is shared. Context fills in the Technicolor details of an otherwise black-and-white and distant story. It makes the story *mine*. It brings the narrative altitude down from 30,000 feet to somewhere closer to 0. In these places, the story touches down and begins to have personal meaning. While Samuel laid out the content of his story in a quick 10 minutes, we spent countless hours talking through the context of what it was like being him in the midst of the tragic events. Content is usually fast. Context slows us down to attune us to the experience.

Men are creatures of content. We often think linearly, wanting to go step-by-step through a story in anticipation of the end. Much like an airplane, we find 30,000 feet to be a safety zone, where the mutual lack of oxygen allows us to maintain our distance without the expectation of true engagement. The empty itinerary suffices, and we allow ourselves to hop from topic to tragic topic without ever touching ground. Many believe that if they share enough content, other men will magically understand. But the more we talk *about* the story, the more we keep ourselves and others from feeling it.

True engagement with the tragic story of this abused young man has far less to do with the sequence of events in his life or his baseball bat triumph and much more to do with the experience of *what it was like to be him* in those moments.

Content asks, "Was it a wooden bat or a metal one?" or "How far did you chase him?" or "Did you ever see that man again? What happened to your mother?"

Context, on the other hand, asks, "What was it like to chase your abuser away?" or "How have you had to chase evil in other areas of your life?" and "What does that situation reveal about the deeper story of your life?" More on this in the next chapter.

## BROTHERS AND STORY

The story engagement of brothers is different. Rather than men standing around a barbecue grill making small talk while the beer gets warm and the burgers sizzle, brothers do not settle for the mediocrity of 30,000-foot itineraries told with adept aloofness to prevent others from peering too deeply into the soul. Brothers listen more for context than content and pursue the hearts of one another in the tumult of tragedy and struggle.

The fact is, most men don't do this, but not because we do not want to. It is far more because we don't know how to engage like this. Men don't often risk sharing their stories in such a way as to reveal the depth of their pain. It is far easier to brush off or deny parts of the story than it is to feel the searing yet redemptive presence of another man at ground zero in our private tragedies. We feel weak, seen, confused, young, and desperately alone. But the most healing place for men to engage is at the very base of our stories. For men to become men through other men, we need an honest retelling of our stories in the presence of other men who will listen, engage, honor, and bless the struggle. We need to shift the focus of our conversation from content to context so that we can begin the process of seeing and knowing one another's stories without the façade of machismo or fear of shame.

Over the past several years, some "men's groups" have focused on the itinerary-level engagement of a man's story. In all honesty, it is a move in the right direction, away from the focus on information toward an awareness of the story. But "to share your story" in these contexts has merely meant the sharing of general themes and biographical information: where you grew up, what your family of origin was like, where you went to school, and so on. It is a mere itinerary of your life, not the real story.

Other groups that ask men to "share their stories" use it as the code word for the confession of sin. Words like "story," "struggle," and "testimony" are subtle ways of inviting men in the group to voyeuristically normalize their own failures by hearing the details of yours. And yes, it can be encouraging to hear how one man faced his sin and found methods to change, but until and unless we enter the actual narratives of his life that led him across the threshold into sin, we completely miss his heart. Groups such as this find story sharing cathartic, but in the end, no one is invited to actual healing.

I believe it is time to go deeper, where men gather in a masculine space and tell one another their stories of innocence, tragedy, struggle, and restoration at a ground level where their hearts actually show up. We must first know our stories, and then we must bring them to other men. It is in this space that we are men together. The scriptures do not spare us the gory and glorious details of men's stories. Why should we not do the same?

## IMPORTANT NOTE

As your group enters this next portion of *Brotherhood Primer,* you will be investigating your own story as well as the stories of the other men. A few words of caution and advice:

1. The following questions give you specific instructions about how to investigate your own story. The more you put into this honest and prayerful reflection of your narrative, the more you will get out of it.

2. No one is required to share. If you are not ready to share your story with the others in the group, simply call a "pass." There is little that is more destructive to the story process than forcing its telling. Honor yourself in this process.

3. These weeks, more than ever, refrain from giving advice, offering fix-it solutions, or really saying much at all. Stories are meant to be heard, not corrected. Read the next chapter on how to listen to stories, and make sure to engage the stories shared from a *context* perspective rather than *content*.

4. You may need several weeks for everyone to share his story. You may have noticed that this is a 10- to 16-week process. Here is where the extra weeks come in. Plan now to give each man roughly 45 minutes to share his story. This translates into *maybe* two men sharing their stories per gathering. Most groups have set aside a whole session for each man to share. Don't rush the experience of being together in the context of your narrative.

5. This is not "accountability" sharing. It's not baring your soul and your deepest, darkest sins. While that may be part of it, the greater exercise is for you to honestly bring your story to other men and have them listen and engage with your context.

Be bold. Be brave. Honor yourself and your story. It deserves to be told.

## PERSONAL REFLECTION

- What is your gut reaction to the content of this chapter? Do you get it? What makes sense? What is confusing?
- In what way is the idea of story challenging you?
- Take a piece of blank paper and create a Story Timeline, plotting out some of the primary experiences in your life using the instructions below. (See example at the end of the chapter.)
- For each of the peaks or valleys on your timeline, write a few sentences that reveal more about the context. What was your experience like at that moment? What was lost? What was shattered? What hope was renewed?
- Look at the moments of tragedy on your timeline. How do you see those tragedies connected to significant areas of struggle in your life today?
- What messages, themes, or vows have formed in your heart as a result of those experiences? (i.e. I will never trust again. I am all alone. I have to fight my own way through.)
- When you tell your story in the future, what new awareness will you have? How will you tell it?
- As you listen to stories shared by men in the future, how will you now listen and engage them?
- Spend a few moments thinking about the future God-directed restoration. Notice parts of your heart that soar and those places where doubt, cynicism, and anger enter. Describe your hope and your fear.

Instructions for Story Timeline

1. Lay out a timeline of significant events from your birth until about 18 years old. Though you are likely older than 18, the most shaping experiences of our stories occur in the earliest years of our lives. Therefore, stop at age 18.
2. Plot the highlight moments, those times when you knew goodness and life, on the top half of the page. The more life you experienced, the higher above the line.
3. Plot the tragic moments, those times when you knew wounding and trauma, on the bottom half. The more devastating the experience, the lower you put it.
4. You may have either good or traumatic "seasons," where there are far too many moments to plot individually. That's okay. Simply mark them as a season. For example, "Grandma moved in" might be a highlight that covers a year of your life. Or "Coach Smith" may represent a season of great harm that spans the entirety of sixth grade.
5. Now, go back and consider the four aspects of story: innocence, tragedy, struggle, and restoration. How would you like to represent those on your timeline?
6. Clearly mark the tragedies with a "T" or "t."
7. Did you miss anything significant? Are you avoiding anything?
8. Ask the Lord for further insight into your story with regard to content versus context.

## GROUP DISCUSSION

- Do not yet share your stories in the group. There will be time for that in the coming weeks. For now, spend some time talking about the process.
- What was it like for you to create a timeline of 0-18 years old? What did you notice about your own thoughts and feelings as you put things down on paper?
- Where did you find yourself either angry or tender? What made you mad to remember? What broke your heart?
- When you consider sharing some of these things with the group in the future, what fear and/or excitement arises?
- How do you find yourself judging your story (i.e. it's too much for others to handle, or it's not really that tragic after all)?
- What do you need the other men in the group to know about how you are engaging this process? What do you need from them when it comes time to share your story?

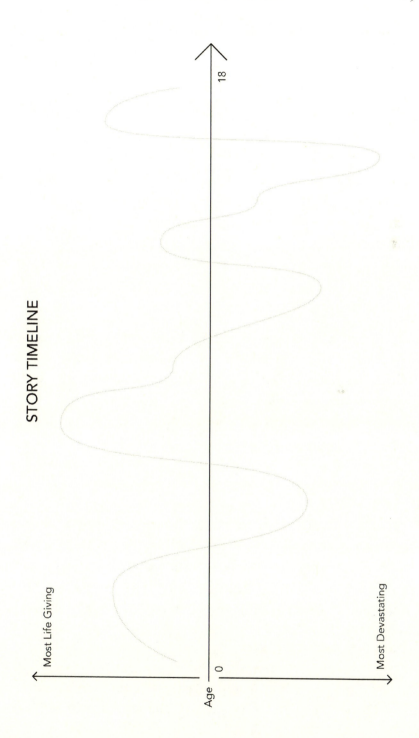

# 6

# WHAT'S YOUR STORY? PART II

In early June 2012, along the northern foothills of the Colorado Rocky Mountains, a lightning bolt found its way to the dry undergrowth of the forest. Crackly pine needles spurred by the relentless gusts of downslope winds transformed the spark into a flame. As minutes turned to hours, and hours to days, the blaze engulfed a total of 87,415 acres of both National Forest and private land, destroyed 250 homes, and killed one person. To this day, it is known as "one of the largest and most destructive wildfires in Colorado history."[1]

Along with many other Northern Colorado residents, I drove to the safe edge of the fire to witness the blaze. I sat 15 miles away on the hood of my car with two of my children, inundated by the smell of smoke in the air. The haze hung over our little town like a blanket. Large plumes rose up like atomic mushroom clouds overhead as helicopters and tanker planes criss-crossed back and forth in their attempts to douse the flames.

In many ways, life in our city of Fort Collins, Colorado, carried on. Kids played in the neighborhood pool. The trash truck wound its way through the streets. People found their way to work and back, and the clock tick-tocked its way through the day. Yet a sad solemnity covered the Front Range, just as the sky turned from its normal brilliant Colorado blue to a gray-brown haze. A shadow covered our world, a blanket of disaster that everyone recognized and knew, yet tried desperately to deny. Ever since then, I am acutely aware of anything approximating the smell of smoke, horrified to think more devastation such as this could be possible in our pristine corner of the world. The fact is, since then, wildfire has returned many times, and we mourn the loss of beauty every single time.

From the moment of the Fall in Genesis 3, when Adam and Eve succumbed to the temptation to "be like God," a similar shadow has been cast over all of humanity. Like the spreading doom of Mordor, sin and fallenness consume everything in their path. There is 0% containment, and no matter what religious effort may be set against them, nothing on earth can stop them. Innocence has been lost, shalom has been shattered, and our return to Eden has forever been blocked. Once we passed the threshold of Genesis 3, there was no turning back. We now struggle to live in a world of shadow.

The shadow is easy to see. It hangs over every person, every relationship, every beautiful thing. It fills our minds and our hearts, invades our dreams, and obliterates our hopes. It is everywhere. Racism. Debt. Genocide. Poverty. Abuse. Depression. Fraud. Cancer. Politics. Stubbed toes. Trafficking. Sitcoms. Fatherlessness. Sibling rivalry. Pornography. Alzheimer's. Greed. Infertility. Theft. False religions. Misogyny. Misandry. Hate. Debt. Lust. Anger. Gluttony. The list is endless. It fills the sky and shrouds all who attempt to go about their daily lives with any glimmer of hope.

The good news is this was never how we were *meant* to be.

## GLORY: THE FIRST STORY

What we were meant to be is so ancient and so mythic it has become a part of the past that rarely finds its way into the present. Before the shadowfall came God's poetic and glorious creation. His intention for all humanity is and has always been to reflect His glory as His image bearers on earth.

Consider again Genesis 1:27: "So God created mankind in his own image, in the image of God he created them; male and female he created them."[2]

No other creature or created thing receives this kind of crowing. Humanity alone is endowed with the glory of his likeness. As the pinnacle of creation, men and women receive from God the ultimate honor. The writer of Genesis believes this fact is of such importance, and that it remains true even after the horrifying events of Genesis 3, he repeats himself in Genesis 5:1 saying, "When God created mankind, he made them in the likeness of God."[3]

Thousands of years later, the Apostle Paul[4] also remains adamant about this most important fact. In Ephesians 1 and 2, he expounds even more. He tells us of the time before time, "before the creation of the world,"[5] when God delights in the very thought of each one of us, His image-bearing sons and daughters, and determines to set the course of history such that each of us would exist in order to reflect His glory. In chapter 2, he tells us, "For we are God's handiwork, created in Christ Jesus to do good works, which God prepared in advance for us to do."[6] Astounding. According to Paul, humanity is the *handiwork* of God. Other English translations use words like craftsmanship, workmanship, and masterpiece. Indeed, Paul uses a fascinating Greek word here, *poeima*. This is where we get our English words for "poem" and "poetry."

God is a poet.

Consider this for a moment: Before the beginning of time, despite His omniscient awareness of the shadow that is to come, the delight of God rests so fully on the creation of His image bearers He determines *even then* to craft/create/*poet* each of us into existence, in the creative love and restorative power of Jesus, in order to bring His goodness to the world. Read that sentence again.

This, my friend, is what I call your *first story*. It is the original story, the deeper story, the story God has been telling about you from before time even began. This is the most true story about you.

In order for us to find our place in the greater metanarrative of God, we must return to God's original intent, purpose, and design for all of us. We have completely forgotten we were not made for this fallen world, and we have settled into the cadence of ambivalent living as if we were nothing more than automatons. The only way to break free is to remember something different.

In *The Lion, the Witch and the Wardrobe*, the Christ figure named Aslan returns to life after having laid his down on behalf of another. Author C.S. Lewis provides us with a glimpse of what is meant by the original pre-Fall glory. When asked what the resurrection means, he responds,

> "It means," said Aslan, "that though the Witch knew the Deep Magic, there is a *magic deeper still* which she did not know. Her knowledge goes back only to the dawn of time. But if she could have looked a little farther back, into the stillness and the darkness before Time dawned, she would have read there a different incantation."[7]

A magic deeper still. You see, *before* the Fall, *before* the apple, *before* the shadow, *before* hiding in the bushes, *before* sin and death and tragedy came something far more epic, far more weighty, and far more difficult to comprehend: *glory*. We have lost touch with God's original intention for us. Our focus has become shadow management, and our hearts have lost hope of ever living as God originally designed.

We have forgotten who we really are. We have forgotten the reality of our sin is not the most true part of us. Indeed, we all now exist outside of Eden, and as a result, every human who has ever lived is born separated from relationship with God. But God did not intend or design us that way. His glorious intention for us lives in us still, and in order to find it, we must return, as Lewis says, "into the stillness and the darkness before Time dawned."

In another of Lewis's writings, he admonishes us to consider our fellow humans as bearers of this divine glory. He writes, "There are no 'ordinary' people. You have never talked to a mere mortal."[8] Every human bears the glorious image of God and is intended by God to live according to this first story.

## SHADOW: THE SECOND STORY

But we don't. We can't. We have been exiled from our Edenic home and live outside of innocence. As with our original parents, our eyes have been opened to our brokenness and nakedness, and we have shifted our focus from God's heart to our own self-preservation.

You see, we have an enemy, and we were born into battle, a battle of clashing stories. The enemy of God wants nothing more than to dethrone Him and mar His face. As a lesser being with lesser power, he can do no such thing; therefore, he turns his violence against all of creation, reserving his most vehement assault for those who most fully reflect God's glory: humanity. His aim is to steal, kill, and destroy everything in his path, and he spreads his shadow across the whole world and over every human heart.

*The second story becomes the narrative we most believe about ourselves, and like echoes of a far and distant past, we can no longer remember we are sons and daughters of a good and glorious King.*

This is what I call the *second story*. It is written by the enemy of our souls as he seeks to overwrite and eradicate the first story, our story of glory. He launches his attack against God's image bearers with both specificity and relentlessness. Of God's masterpiece in each one of us, he smashes and slashes, shatters and smatters, until the wounding, trauma, tragedy, and pain of our experience begins to overcome and define us. The second story becomes the narrative we most believe about ourselves, and like echoes of a far and distant past, we can no longer remember we are sons and daughters of a good and glorious King.

Yet despite the enemy's most vicious efforts, he does not have the power to either create or uncreate. That which God has made cannot be unmade. Therefore, though shadow and marring have come against us in the form of trauma and tragedy, the image-bearing poetic masterpiece remains under the rubble of our second stories. It is in the context of deep and honest connection with others, who witness our lives and help us sift through the debris of our stories, that we can begin to recover and reclaim the inheritance of our first stories once again. This is the ultimate purpose of brotherhood.

When my kids were younger, they loved watching *The Lion King*. All three of them would immediately scramble to the couch the moment we mentioned the film. Even to this day, over a decade later as mostly adults, they will collectively and spontaneously erupt with fervent and passionate voices into the songs from the movie. After shuffling through the music, they then start to quote, verbatim, the various memorable lines from the show. Their dramatic recreation almost always culminates in a re-enactment of the most important moment of Simba's storyline.

As Simba speaks to the ghost of his father, Mufasa says: "You have forgotten who you are and so have forgotten me. Look inside yourself, Simba. You are more than what you have become. You must take your place in the circle of life."

Simba retorts, "How can I go back? I'm not who I used to be."

To which Mufasa's ghost responds, "Remember who you are. You are my son and the one true king. Remember who you are."[9]

Yes, we must all remember who we are. Our second stories have attempted to convince us of a narrative we were never designed to live. We have fallen into a collective amnesia, and we need other men to peer into the depths of our stories, hear about the moments of shattered innocence and painful wounding, and then lift our eyes to the deeper story we have long forgotten. True masculine accountability is not to help us avoid sin. No, real accountability is when brothers remind us of our first story, who we actually are, and then call us forth to live from that place. We cannot see our own face, so we need our brothers to reflect back to us how we each uniquely bear the image of God.

As we enter and engage the sharing of our stories with other men, we must have keen eyes for the evidence of the Creator. Every one of us is designed, intended, and marked by God, and it is our task as a collective of men to discover it once again.

## THE MARKINGS OF GOD

Several years ago I traveled to the southern coast of Turkey, right along the Mediterranean Sea. Thirty or so ministry leaders from around the world gathered together in a beachfront hotel, all seeking camaraderie and rejuvenation from an assembly of like-minded believers. I had the privilege of creating the space for us to turn toward God, ourselves, and others in soulful reflection.

Representing 14 different nationalities, our diverse group was asked to empty their pockets onto the tables around which they sat. I instructed them to examine the coins they produced and to indicate to the larger group what they found emblazoned on them. As you can imagine, with people from 14 different passport countries serving the Kingdom in at least 25 countries around the world, the sheer diversity of coinage that clanged on the table far exceeded my expectations. As we examined the money, we found that regardless of country of origin, three themes emerged. Each coin indicated its *value*. Each coin identified its *home*. And every piece of currency bore an *image* of an important person.

In the ancient Near East, the term for *character* developed from the process of engraving. A simple piece of metal would be transformed through an emblazoning process by which it would be "characterized" with these three important indicators of value, belonging, and identity. Thereafter, each coin, no matter where in the world it went or in whose possession it remained, held on its face the reflection of its original story.

As image bearers, representatives of the I AM God on earth, our *character* as humans is directly tied to the *value*, *home* and *image* we bear. You see, our glory is not about us, but about the One from whom we get our name.[10] We do not belong here, but are sojourners in a foreign land. Indeed, over time and with use, the coin is bent, marked, and marred, and it may travel great distances and be used for countless purposes, but the original *character* is never lost. It will forever be emblazoned with the markings of its origin.[11]

## VALUE

A few moments ago, my wife emerged from the laundry room with a few crumpled pieces of dripping wet paper. She gently laid them on the table next to me. Last night, in the late-night rush to hit the sack, I dropped my jeans on the floor without emptying the pockets. Good husband that I am, I made sure to get them into the laundry basket this morning.

Now, two $20 bills sit beside me. They have seen better days. Before daring to use them, I might need to iron them or something. But the fact is, their *value* does not stem from their condition, but is inherent in their existence. $20 is $20, crumpled and wet or not.

It is the same with humans. Our value does not come from the material from which we were made. Are we not merely flesh and bone, just like every other creature who walks the earth? The value of humanity, and of each and every divinely poeted person to ever exist, derives from the One who gives it value. Just as the value of a $20 bill is determined by an external authority, the U.S. government, so too every human's value is determined by the Creator.

Regardless of how the enemy has sought to write a second story by bringing direct and repetitive assaults against your life, whether through capital "T" or little "t" tragedies, he cannot ultimately eradicate your value, because your value comes from someone who cannot be destroyed. The first story value remains emblazoned on your being, even if you find yourself crumpled, wet, torn, or defaced.

## HOME

In that conference room on the Mediterranean coast, people from 14 nations produced coinage from 30+ countries. The key to understanding that last sentence is the word "from." The peso is *from* Mexico. The yen is *from* Japan. The lira is *from* Turkey. The manat is *from* Azerbaijan. Every piece of currency clearly states its origin. No matter how far and wide it travels, its home never changes.

The scriptures tell us humans were created for a different home than we now inhabit. While the post-Eden earth is now our residence, it is apparently not our home. Consider the following passage:

> All these people were still living by faith when they died. They did not receive the things promised; they only saw them and welcomed them from a distance, admitting that they were foreigners and strangers on earth. People who say such things show that they are looking for a country of their own. If they had been thinking of the country they had left, they would have had opportunity to return. Instead, they were longing for a better country—a heavenly one. Therefore God is not ashamed to be called their God, for he has prepared a city for them.[12]

Written into the very etchings of our character is an *elsewhere* citizenship. We belong to a Kingdom that is completely "other." Our potential and our glory derive not from our birthplace, but from our King's place.

## IMAGE

No one has seen the face of God. Moses tried, but out of God's mercy, he only saw His back.[13] The priest in *Indiana Jones* looked into the ark and beheld something glorious, and then his face melted like hot wax.

What, then, does it mean to bear His image or to be made in His likeness?

Imprinted onto every one of the coins on those tables was a face—not the *actual* face of the individual, but a representation of him or her. Someone famous, important, powerful, or beautiful can be found on the "heads" side of every coin. And because of that emblazoned image, the coin has meaning.

Several years ago, while my wife and I attended graduate school, we scrounged and scrimped and struggled to make ends meet. After moving back to the United States from living as overseas missionaries, we rediscovered some old coins left to me by my grandmother. An assortment of vintage pennies spanning a hundred years of American history, we figured they might be worth something. And they were.

Well, some of them at least.

I took them to the coin guy down the street. With each one, he meticulously separated and researched, referenced and recorded the value, date, and meaning of each one. "What meaning does a penny have?" you might ask. The meaning is derived from the visage on its head.

Despite their age, some were worth a mere cent. Other pennies were valued at ten dollars or more. In the lexicon of coins, faces apparently make a world of difference. Whose face the coin bears is of utmost importance. Not only has God emblazoned on you your value and your home, He has given to each one of His image bearers His own face. We have meaning because we reflect Him. His face in ours. And like a trillion-sided diamond, we each bear His image in our own uniquely and divinely inspired way. No masterpiece is the same, though we are all part of the same collection made by the same artist. The purpose of the masterpiece is to reveal the Master.

Our challenge is to view one another and ourselves through the lens of *value, home,* and *image* rather than under the shadow of our second stories. As I have already said, "There are no 'ordinary' people."[14] That includes you.

I have written far more extensively about the concepts of first and second story in *Sage: A Man's Guide Into His Second Passage.*[15] You can find it on Amazon.com.

## PERSONAL REFLECTION

- What stands out to you in this chapter? What clicks, and what do you wonder about?
- How do the concepts of first story and second story land with you? Are you able to see them at work in your own life?
- What can you note in regard to your second story? How were you told "who" to be?
- What might it look like for you to honor the loss of what was intended? To grieve your second story?
- Go back to your 0-18 year old timeline. As you look over it, consider the concepts of first and second story. Where do you see evidence of the first? Where do you see the shadow of your second story start to take shape?
- What happens in your mind/heart/spirit when you consider there is a "story deeper still" within you?
- In what ways can you begin to identify how you have attempted to survive the second story?

## GROUP DISCUSSION

- Do not yet share your stories with one another. We are working toward this, so hold tight.
- How do your perspectives of one another change when you consider that each of you has a first story older than the second story? How do your perspectives about yourselves change?
- What do you imagine shifting in your relationships and discussions if this is the case?
- How does the understanding and experience of authenticity and vulnerability in your group change when you consider each man's first and second story?

- Why is it important to have other men know our stories, both the first and the second stories?
- Value, home, and image. How do those concepts land with you? Why do you think this is an important orientation before we begin to share stories with one another?

# 7
# HOW TO ENGAGE A MAN'S STORY

We have all met him. You know who I am talking about. Let's call him Gary.[1]

Together, with three other men, we sat with Gary at a Starbucks at an early morning gathering. Acquaintances from a past life, we reunited after years of no contact, looking forward to reconnecting and hearing how everyone was doing. Having battled in the ministry trenches together for years, we still felt an affection and affinity for one another although it had been a long time.

After the initial high-level flyover where each of us provided some brief and basic demographic information about our current lives, the conversation turned toward deeper matters. As one man began to share about the significant challenges he faced in his career and marriage, tears formed in the corners of his eyes. He had held it in for years, not having anyone close enough or present enough to unveil his pain. But, just as he was about to take an even deeper dive into his story, Gary leaned over, patted him on the shoulder, and said, "You shouldn't feel bad, man. God's got you. I was in the exact same place. I went back to school to get re-certified, started marriage counseling, and *voila*, here I am, loving life."

Shoot. Me. Now.

You can predict what happened. The man who was sharing did a complete reversal, pulling up and out of the depths he had started to plummet. His tears instantly dried up, and I could see him swallow deeply. Without skipping a beat, Gary continued talking, completely hijacking the conversation as he detailed to the rest of us the steps he took to transform his life. Though he did not seem to notice, everyone leaned back, crossed arms, and started looking at the time. In that moment, I thanked God I ordered the venti coffee instead of the tall, for it gave me an excuse to get up and use the bathroom. Upon my return, Gary was *still* talking, and everyone else suddenly had to run off to meetings.

Gary. Of course, I write this with an edge of extreme, but believe me, it is not far from the truth. We have all met and experienced this type of man. The deeper truth is, we have all *been* this man at one time or another. As Martin Luther King, Jr., says, "We have learned to fly the air like birds and swim the sea like fish, but we have not learned the simple art of living together as brothers."[2] As we dive further into the process of developing an intentional brotherhood with one another, we must learn not only how to *share* our stories, but how to *listen* to them as well.

> *The landscape of a man's heart is sacred, and when he begins to open the door to invite us in, we must take off our shoes and enter as if we were entering a holy sanctuary.*

We are unfortunately trained as men to continually measure each other up, to compare ourselves with one another, and to strive to look good and gain the other men's respect and approval. One-upmanship is a thing, and we must be acutely aware of our tendency to default to it. To truly be with another man as he shares his story means we are actually *with* him, rather than thinking about what we will say next, what story of ours we will share, or how we have experienced (or not) similar circumstances. The landscape of a man's heart is sacred, and when he begins to open the door to invite us in, we must take off our shoes and enter as if we were entering a holy sanctuary. There are far too many "Garys" in the world. It's time to make the shift toward brother.

## I AND THOU

Jewish philosopher Martin Buber famously framed human-to-human relationships in the following three categories: 1) It - It; 2) I - It; and 3) I - Thou.

Along with several other theologians and thinkers, Buber's philosophy is based on the biblical foundation of the *imago Dei*, or the "image of God" written into the life and story of every human being. He believed every person uniquely and divinely reflects the Maker and, therefore, holds within his or her being a divine "*I*". In essence, *I* exist because God exists, and *I* am created with divine purpose and intention. Therefore, every *I* is worthy of acknowledgement and pursuit. Each person is called by God to hold closely and tenderly his or her own *I* in order to be in relational connection with one another. When this occurs, and my *I* can engage with your divine *I*, I now experience your *Thou*. Rather than viewing the other as an object, the goodness of the *I - Thou* relationship is established. Both parties are seen and experienced as image bearers.

In his nomenclature, an *"It"* is viewed and experienced as an object. *It* merely serves a function, has no existential or metanarrative purpose, and makes no impact. As a simple example, every time we go to the grocery store, the buyer and the checkout person engage as *Its* together: I have a function—to make it through the transaction by giving some money for the items I want—and the checkout person's function is to scan the items and collect the appropriate amount from me. There is no deeper engagement and no deeper impact other than to successfully buy and sell groceries. Though it may involve a human-to-human exchange, it might as well be a self-checkout. We have been in an *It - It* encounter. It works, it's functional, and it is so very disconnected and lonely.

When one person offers his *I* but the other person does not, the result is an *I - It* exchange. The truth is, we *It* ourselves and each other all the time. A hundred times a day we engage with other people from a posture of "othering," whether it is toward another or reflectively back toward ourselves. Living in this post-Edenic world, we only catch glimpses of *I - Thou* relating. Yet it is in these moments of deep connection where healing and hope are found.

As a brotherhood of men, our task is to intentionally unlearn our past habits of *It'ing* ourselves and one another. One-upmanship is nothing more than *It'ing*. We are black belts at "othering," completely missing the deep and core reflection of God buried in the very fabric of our image-bearing humanity. And so, we far too often settle for men's experiences of *It - It* because we have lost all sense of what else is possible.

As a man shares his story, it is vital for us to shift our posture to one of *I - Thou*. Jesus Himself says, "For where two or three gather in my name (i.e. in the midst of the Divine where two *I's* exist), there am I with them."[3] God shows up in the in-between of human engagement. And I am convinced we all want God to show up.

## THREE CRUCIAL POSTURES

Gary defaults into three connection-breaking postures.

First, Gary is oblivious. Maybe it is intentional, maybe it is not, but the net result is the killing of connection. He seems completely unaware of what is unfolding in front of him. His self-focus drives him away from others while posing as a means to build connection. He is highly committed to talking about himself, believing when he does he increases the likelihood of building bridges and establishing a library of shared experiences through which others can relate. While his desire is for relationship, his unawareness of the other man creates instead an *It - It* exchange. He is *It'ing* himself and the other guy simultaneously.

When this occurs, we feel the collective departure from the Divine. We experience the shift both in the group and in ourselves, where alarms start blaring and the red flags wave wild. Rather than creating a space where vulnerability, risk, and a true heart can be unveiled, it is now a place of comparison and advice, and no one wants that.

As I have already stated, each of us knows a Gary and each of us has been a Gary. We have experienced both sides of this interaction. As a result, it is incumbent upon us all to grow in our capacity to engage one another from a different posture—to move from obliviousness toward a posture of awareness.

Awareness

Humor me for a moment. Set down the book and close your eyes. Allow the gaze of your mind's eye to survey the world around you, taking in all the information provided to you by your other senses. What do you hear? What do you smell? What do you taste? What do you feel?

I hear the cars passing on the road outside my window, splashing their way through the slush and snow. I also hear the hum of the refrigerator and the faint laughter of children throwing snowballs.

I smell the remainders of this morning's coffee still sitting on my desk, stone cold and unwanted. I can also smell the lingering aroma of lunch hanging in the air, as well as the faint fragrance of the lotion I put on my Colorado-dry hands an hour ago.

I taste the post-lunch beginnings of bad breath, remembering I have gum in my backpack on the floor across the room. I can also already taste the meal I will be having for dinner tonight, looking forward to the tomato sauce that will smother the pasta with all its goodness.

I feel the tightness in my shoulders left over from yesterday's harrowing drive, one that should have taken two hours, but instead took five due to the interstate closure. I feel the burn of my rear end, tired from the chair in which I have spent the day.

Now, turn your attention to your internal world, and wonder what of your experience might simply be waiting for your awareness. What do you notice about how you are? What words would you use to describe your heart right now?

I notice a tinge of anxiety as I anticipate three meetings I have later this afternoon. I am aware of my body's battery starting to edge toward yellow, as I have already been awake for 10 hours today, and it's only 2 p.m. in the afternoon. I find myself wondering what my wife is doing right now. But more importantly, I wonder *how* she is doing with all she has on her plate.

The fact is, we can only be as aware of others as we are of our own selves.

When we are listening to and engaging another person, the posture of awareness opens the space for an *I - Thou* experience. We are able to step out of ourselves in order to marvel at the image bearer in front of us. We can listen without the burning need to prove anything, be anything, or say anything. We become aware not only of the story the individual is sharing, but of all of the underlying communication not offered with words.

We see the way his face twists and contorts every time he mentions his father.

We hear the tone of his voice as he bravely brings words to his internal experience.

We feel his fear and his hope of offering himself so vulnerably.

We notice his word choices, his cadence, and his abrupt halt when he talks about his tragedies.

Awareness is the first vital posture we must learn to take when engaging the stories of others. Whether it is the men in your Brotherhood group, your wife or girlfriend, your children, your coworkers, or even the clerk at the checkout counter, awareness is the key that unlocks the possibility of a different kind of engagement.

Curiosity

Once we become aware, we have a choice: to make assumptions and judgments or to move toward curiosity.

For most of us, we default toward assumption. It is actually quite natural for our brains to form neurological pathways born from our previous experiences in order to provide a capacity to anticipate the future. If I were to tell you, "Let's go out for steak tonight," you would likely make assumptions about what you might expect the dinner experience to be like. Your mind draws from your previous experiences of steak, including the type of restaurant, the taste of the meat, the way you like it cooked, and even what selection of sides you may encounter on the menu. Your past informs your anticipation of the future, making connections with historical data points to provide you with the greatest possibility of a good meal the next time.

Simultaneous to your assumptions are your judgments. You prefer this steakhouse over that one. You prefer not to eat steak tonight because you know you are grilling them tomorrow. Beyond the actual food, you make other judgments as well. For example, you might think it is a great idea to go out tonight to celebrate or it is a terrible idea since you are trying to be more budget conscious this year. Regardless, the simple invitation to a steak dinner is immediately accompanied by a host of assumptions and judgments. It is simply the way we operate.

When we enter the realm of story, however, we need to check our assumptions and judgments at the door and instead move toward curiosity. This is crucial, making a significant difference in the engagement between people. Noting what we have become aware of, both in ourselves and in the storyteller, we open our thoughts to curiosity rather than jumping to conclusions, which is a classic Gary move.

Is it not fascinating to observe the way Jesus interacts with people throughout His ministry? Though He is the omniscient God who knows all things, His first engagements with people much of the time are questions rather than statements. He asks, and in His asking, He opens the door to a much more significant conversation and interaction.

You see, there are two types of questions. The first and most basic question seeks more information. It pursues details and specifics, and it lives in the realm of content. The second kind of question focuses on context, where humans live. It wonders about the experience, the feelings, the perspectives, the interpretations, and, ultimately, the heart. When we move from awareness to curiosity, the more impactful and more helpful questions center around the context. In fact, context is only discovered through awareness and curiosity.

After being invited into the sacred landscape of story with another man, we set aside our one-upmanship, lay down our need to be right or helpful or insightful, step away from how his story reminds us of a sermon we once heard or a book he should read, and stay *with him*. Through our awareness of what he is bringing, we move toward curiosity, allowing us to wonder about the unexplored and unnamed territory we have just entered. It is a classic Jesus move, and it makes all the difference.

Curt Thompson writes, "We are all born into the world looking for someone looking for us."[4] As I have already said, each one of us is desperate to be seen but terrified of being found. When a man begins to open his life and story to others, he is risking the exposure of his heart in the hope someone will see and find him. Awareness and curiosity form the first two postures we must take if we are ever to truly find one another. Otherwise, we remain at a 30,000-foot relational altitude and merely skim the surface of God's goodness, which is written onto our hearts.

The key to curious engagement is compassion and empathy. Much has been written about these qualities, and I encourage you to become a student of both. The more compassionate and empathetic of a man you can become, the deeper and more rich your relationships of all kinds will become. Yet they are not the topics men's ministry material typically addresses. More often, we are told to be strong, protective, stalwart, determined, unmoveable, and so on. As a result, men are trained to only live half of God's purpose for true masculine engagement.

Compassion has two parts. Similar to the meaning of *con-* in confidence, *com-* means to be with, to share, to enter in with another. Though we may often assume *passion* is related to desire, the deeper meaning has far more to do with suffering. Consider the phrase "the passion of the Christ" in reference to the final week of Jesus's life as He moves toward the cross and crucifixion. *Compassion*, therefore, means to suffer *with* another. Whereas pity may involve a general sense of tenderness, it both stays at a distance and maintains a level of power differential.[5] Compassion is an *I - Thou* exchange between people. It says, "I see you, I see your suffering, and I join you there and validate your suffering as an equal." Compassion is what we are called to offer others in the midst of their pain.

Similar to compassion, empathy is the currency of connectedness between two people. According to Brene Brown, empathy involves four specific qualities: *perspective taking*, where we are able to take the perspective of another person and see the world and story through his or her eyes; *being non-judgmental*, where we refrain from jumping to our own conclusions; *recognizing emotion*, where we are aware of the other person's feelings; and *communicating our awareness to them*. Brown says, "Empathy is feeling *with* people."[6]

If you are anything like me, training in compassion and empathy was not part of my upbringing as a boy. It has not been part of most men's ministry experiences I have had, nor have I ever heard of someone being referred to as a "man's man" who overtly displays compassion and empathy as his strongest qualities. However, true and deep connection with others can only be found when compassion and empathy are present. It is no wonder we find ourselves in such desperate and isolated states.

As a man shares his story, he first needs the listeners to be aware of him and what he's bringing. Moreover, he needs brothers to be aware of *how* he is telling his story. He cannot see his own face, and he cannot hear his own voice. He needs brothers to listen to his tone of voice, notice his strained shoulders, watch his eyes for tears, and be aware of the words he chooses as he shares. Then, when awareness exists, those same brothers have the opportunity to respond with curiosity.

The third posture crucial for a story listener to take is the posture of kindness.

Kindness

Psalm 62 says this: "Power belongs to you, God, and with you, Lord, is unfailing love."[7] Within God's very being exist two seemingly opposite realities, power and love. Other translations use strength or might and mercy, tenderness, or lovingkindness. God is a God of strength and tenderness. He holds within Himself perfectly and equally the might of His being with the gentleness of His presence. This, I believe, is the space of kindness.

Kindness is the intersection of strength and tenderness. It is where the fullness of God's power and might commingle with His compassionate mercy and generosity. Kindness has both a sharp edge and a gentle hand. Kindness is not niceness or politeness. No, kindness holds its ground while simultaneously offering hope.

Paul asks us in Romans 2:4 a very provocative question, "Do you show contempt for the riches of his kindness, forbearance and patience, not realizing that God's kindness is intended to lead you to repentance?"[8] Not His power, not His judgment, not His law, not your obedience, not fear or wrath or anger or demand. It is God's *kindness* that leads us to transformation and change.

Kindness is another word for love.

Consider 1 Corinthians 13:4-8:

Love is patient, love is kind. It does not envy, it does not boast, it is not proud. It does not dishonor others, it is not self-seeking, it is not easily angered, it keeps no record of wrongs. Love does not delight in evil but rejoices with the truth. It always protects, always trusts, always hopes, always perseveres. Love never fails.

When we begin to explore our stories and truly examine the nature of the moments when tragedy and trauma occurred, we will find places where kindness did not exist. Darkness can only live in the absence of kindness. As brothers journeying together into places in our narratives where we have seldom, if ever, gone, we have the opportunity to bring kindness where it has not previously been known.

Awareness leads to curiosity. Curiosity leads to kindness. And kindness leads to transformation and healing.

As men, this is a completely different sort of engagement. True brotherhood not only involves fun, play, and even risky experiences that result in high fives and raised glasses. It also includes significant moments of storytelling and story listening where awareness, curiosity, and kindness forge bonds of deeply masculine relationships. We do not change or grow as a result of information or content. We mature in the crucible of an authentic brotherhood that is far more committed to our *imago Dei* than concerned about our waywardness.

## PERSONAL REFLECTION

- Who is the "Gary" in your life? What has your experience of him been?
- In what ways do you find Gary in you?
- Think about the interactions you had today. Reflect on how they felt, and how you felt in the midst of them. Which ones were *It - It,* and which ones were *I - Thou?* What made the difference?
- After reading through the three core postures of engaging another person (awareness, curiosity, and kindness), which one seems to be the most challenging for you?
- What keeps you from awareness?
- What keeps you from curiosity?
- What keeps you from kindness?
- As you consider sitting with the other men in your group as they share their stories, what do you need to be aware of *for yourself* as you are with them?
- What might it be like for you to have a group of men listen to you this way? What do you need to do to prepare yourself for that?
- Review your 0-18-year-old timeline. What are you aware of? What are you curious about? Where in the story is kindness known or not known?

## GROUP DISCUSSION

- Next week, we will begin sharing our stories with one another. How are you feeling about that?
- How have we, as a group, experienced *It-ing* together? This is not to correct or judge anyone, but to name it so we have the opportunity to grow. What needs to be

addressed in our group dynamic before we begin offering our stories to one another?
- How would you describe awareness? Curiosity? Kindness? Which one is hardest for you?
- As a group, lay out the next several weeks. Decide when each man will share his story. Will one man share each time, or will you try for two? Make sure everyone from the group can be there, and make a commitment to each other to show up on time.
- What is happening in your heart as we approach the story-sharing portion of this group?

———

As you prepare for story sharing, be aware of these five tips:

## 5 TIPS FOR STORY-LISTENERS

As you enter into the story-sharing experience of Brotherhood, here are a few practical tips to help set the stage.

- **Clarify Time:** It is always helpful for everyone in the group to have a sense of time. As you invite a man to share his story, make sure to indicate the amount of time he has to share. It's as simple as asking, "It's 6:30 now. How does 45 minutes sound to you? We'll shoot to be done around 7:15." This gives a level of practical containment for everyone involved.
- **Stay Present:** *Withness* is at the core of relationship. Being *with* one another is crucial for an *I - Thou* engagement. Therefore, stay aware of yourself as you are with your brother, and do what you can to stay with him as he shares. If you find yourself beginning to think about other things, have some curiosity rather than pass

judgment. What is happening for you? Is it as simple as a caffeine crash? Or is his story bringing up things in you that feel unsettling? Take notice, and then return to your brother.

- **Be Aware of the Other Men:** Should another man in the group start to edge toward being the fix-it guy, the advice-giver guy, or the one-upmanship guy (i.e. Gary), take the initiative to gently address him and invite him back to the type of engagement your brotherhood is looking for. In all likelihood, he has no idea that is where he's headed and just needs a kind reminder. It is crucial for other listeners to step in on behalf of the storyteller.

- **Don't Collude with the False Narrative:** When telling our stories, we often subconsciously invite the listener to join us in our judgments and our contempt toward ourselves. As a story listener, be aware of the pull to collude with untruth. Instead, ask, "Where is the innocent boy in the midst of this experience?" Focus on where the *imago Dei* was marred or lost rather than agree with the darkness of the loss or sin.

- **Get Help:** There may be stories in which more skilled and professional help is needed. This does not mean you or your Brotherhood group have failed. It actually means you have succeeded. To be with another man in the depths of his story, and to find those places where he is bleeding out and in need of more intensive care is kindness in action. Recognize with him the care he needs and deserves and, with his permission, assist him in finding that care.[9]

The reality is, God has given us our entire lives to recover and redeem our stories. This work is a lifelong journey, and the more committed we are to pursuing His heart for us together, the more we will be able to plummet the depths and explore the heights together.

Pause reading the book, and share your stories during the upcoming weeks. As you share your stories, consider the following personal reflection questions:

- What was it like for you to hear that man's story?
- What got prompted and/or triggered in you as a result? What did you feel as you listened to him?
- How did hearing his story open up greater awareness of your own?
- In what ways do you need to tend to your own heart this week after hearing his story?
- What do you need to do to further prepare yourself to share your story when it's your turn?

After all the stories have been shared, return to the following chapter.

# 8
## PAIN

It was 9:34 p.m. sometime in late November 2002. For just over a year, I had lived overseas and worked overtime learning the language in order to share the gospel with the people of the largest unreached nation of the world. As an undercover missionary in the Middle East, I lived on thrill and adrenaline, always aware of the covert nature of our work and always looking for ways to dive into deeper conversation in order to talk about Jesus. My top three values in life are adventure, aesthetics, and transformation, so living a clandestine life in this ancient and exotic metropolis for the sake of Christ hit my sweet spot.

In October of that year, our team had relaunched a small student movement with a remnant of a few local believers. In a country of 76 million people, the church consisted of less than 4,000 members. Our primary mission involved sharing Jesus with the 400,000 university students who lived in our megacity. With a team of just eight staff, that meant 50,000 students each. I was either bold or naive, or maybe a bit of both.

Now, a language-ready leader, I had just delivered my first "talk" to a small crowd of young people in an ancient Armenian church, tucked away in the back alleys of one of the oldest parts of the city. Headed home that late November evening, I marveled at God's goodness and floated down the street on my high. I remember thinking, "I was *made* for this!"

What happened next will be forever etched in my memory.

In a city of 17 million people that straddles two continents, the streets continually bustle with crowds. Constant traffic prevents swift commutes, regardless of the time of day or the direction of your journey. Sidewalks and alleyways are always full, and the West's definition of "personal space" has no meaning in this overcrowded city. From the church, I walked about a mile to a minibus, which dropped me at the cross-continental ferry. Thirty minutes later, I arrived amongst throngs of passengers at the country's largest port. Another mile walk home, and I would be safe in the confines of our apartment.

Fixated on my arrival home, and elated with the work of God that evening in the back-alley church, I took no notice of two men sitting on the stoop of a building as I passed by, a mere five minutes from my home. They rose after I passed and quickly came up behind me. One of them called to me, asking for the time. "It's 9:34," I told them confidently as I kept walking. The smaller one gruffly took my left elbow, saying, "Come here." He attempted to lead me around a dark corner while the other one flanked me on the right. The stench of beer and cigarettes hung on their breath as their glazed eyes met mine.

Yanking my arm away from him, I stopped abruptly in the well-lit exterior of the neighborhood bakery. More than a head taller than either of them, I boldly and fiercely asked, "What do you want?" With a defiant glare and a head tilt, one of them delivered an unspoken answer via a quick punch to my thigh and a hasty retreat. "What are you doing?" I yelled after them. But my words fell on deaf ears and a busy yet inattentive street.

The baker, having witnessed the interchange from behind me, asked if I was alright. At first, the only pain I felt was the remnant of the forceful punch to my leg. But upon further inspection, I noticed a small rip in my pants, just below the right pocket. Thinking the man had punched me with a sharp ring, I stepped behind the pastry counter and pulled down my pants to investigate. Within seconds, blood began running down my leg as I discovered a two-inch gash in my thigh. Blanching at the sight of blood, the baker quickly loaded me into a taxi and sent me to the nearest hospital. During the short ride, I applied pressure to the wound, unable to adequately slow the flow of blood. It was the most harrowing taxi ride of my life.

Arriving in the E.R., my mind still processing what had just occurred, I was barely able to translate the experience to the clerk at the intake desk. I quickly found myself stretched out on a gurney. The number of hovering people increased dramatically as the bleeding continued to increase. Soon, orderlies were joined by nurses, nurses were joined by doctors, doctors were joined by surgeons, and surgeons were joined by police. An undercover missionary now on the grid, I learned a new word in my new language. "You've been *stabbed*," said the doctor, as he wheeled me into emergency surgery. That's not a word they teach you in school.

After recovering from the anesthesia, I awoke to the tearful face of my pregnant wife. We hugged yet said little, for little needs to be said when one brushes disaster. Minutes later, the American-trained surgeon, who fortunately possessed enough English to speak intelligently to my foggy, drug-washed mind, informed us that I had indeed been stabbed. The knife sank a full 10 centimeters into the muscle of my thigh, coming within one centimeter of the femoral artery. Had it severed the leg's primary artery, I would have bled out within a few minutes. It did, however, damage other secondary blood vessels, requiring extensive repair and a surgical opening of 10 centimeters wide by 10 centimeters deep. Bald from the shaving and brown with iodine antiseptic, my leg, with its numerous stitches, looked like a scene from a Stephen King movie.

Thankful for the skillful work and English translation, I did not notice the vice grip I had formed over my wife's delicate hand. The anesthesia was wearing off, and the pain of surgery set in. Wherever there is wounding, there is pain.

## THE DEEP AGONY OF SHOULD

For the next several weeks, this high-flying, language-ready missionary leader lay helplessly on a makeshift futon in the middle of our living room. Unable to bend my leg, I circled back and forth between rage and despair.

I raged at the thought that a little street-stoop man could so effectively take me out of the game[1] with one well-placed lunge. I raged at the enemy who targeted our work of bringing the gospel to the unreached. I raged at my own pedestrian unawareness, not having seen the seedy men lurking in the darkness awaiting their prey. I raged at my own body's glacially slow healing, pushing the boundaries of pain to stubbornly walk to the bathroom or adjust my position. With each movement, I was reminded of my wound by white-hot flashes of agony that radiated through every muscle in my thigh. I raged.

And then, within minutes of raging, I would fall into despair as I considered the brevity of life and the reality of my own fragility. Holding my two-year-old son while watching my expecting wife attend to my needs, I fell apart internally. I had been *stabbed*. Even now in the telling, the word feels surreal and distant. A 10-centimeter piece of metal had effectively taken out a six-foot-three-inch man, broken my pride, and reawakened me to the reality of my own humanity. Alone on the futon for hours, I felt the hopelessness of our missional task ransack my mind. I considered the goodness of God in providing a skilled English-speaking doctor in the small hospital in our neighborhood, and I imagined what *might* have happened if he had not been there…or if the knife had hit a mere centimeter to the left.

As a man cycling between rage and despair, an overwhelming sense of "should" attached itself to my heart. I *should* have been able to handle this. I *should* not be in such pain. I *should* get off my duff and get back to work. I *should* be the one serving my pregnant wife, not vice versa. I *should* push through and continue leading this team. I *should* not be such a wuss. I *should* not have ever let this happen. I *should* not even be here in the first place. The cubicle in my previous job as the financial analyst at the Campbell's Soup Company in Chicago felt much, much safer. I *should* have never left to become a missionary. For many men, the first punch of pain is often accompanied by a second upper jab of *should*.

To regain a sense of control and to battle back the onslaught of the *shoulds*, I walked the mile home from the hospital after the stitches came out, a mere month after the incident. I can indeed be a stubborn man.

## TYPES OF PAIN

What I did not recognize was that I had been stabbed in two places.

The first, and most obvious, was the physical stabbing in my leg. The knife created a physical wound in my right thigh. The result of the wound: pain. Searing pain that radiated both upward and downward and paralyzed movement of any kind. The pain continued for weeks, and any movement reinjured and retore the healing muscle. Fortunately, there is strong medication for such physical pain. And, in His great mercy, God designed our bodies to heal and regenerate in order to return to some modicum of normalcy as soon as possible. While the thigh wound has completely healed, a long, thin line of scar tissue stands as a constant reminder and an occasional internal muscle tremor still slows my pace.

The second form of stabbing was far less evident and surfaced only after the initial trauma subsided. It was a deep stab wound to my soul. That man's knife severed something deep within, as though tearing away or emasculating a portion of my heart that felt strong and invincible, larger-than-life and manly. As I lay on that futon, I felt my heart withering and the emotional distance between myself and those I loved growing ever wider.

I had failed. I could not lead. I could not protect. I could not be the man I had always thought I was. I was less-than. My once-confident demeanor shifted into a more hesitant and unsure stance. *This* was the pain I could not bear. And even now after my leg has fully healed, *this* is the pain that lingers still in my heart and echoes again and again any time I feel thwarted, cut down, or unsure.

Pain is the indicator of wounding. Physical pain tells us where our body has experienced physical trauma. In the same way, emotional and soul-level pain points to the places in our stories where we have experienced emotional trauma. If you are curious about your stories of trauma, follow the pain, for there you will find the wound.

> *If you are curious about your stories of trauma, follow the pain, for there you will find the wound.*

While we cannot do much to control or withstand the wounding, we *do* have a choice about how we will respond to pain.

## POWER UP AND POWER DOWN

In the face of pain, especially the kind of internal, soul-level pain men are reluctant to acknowledge or name, we tend to respond in one of two ways.

Hollywood glorifies the first response for men especially. It is the quintessential "push through" macho response to pain. I call it "power up." When something hurts, powering up calls you to face it, grit your teeth, put your shoulder into it, and give it a good, hard push. In order to deal with pain, men often find ways to emotionally anesthetize it in order to not let it get the better of them. When threatened by infirmity or pain, men tend to power up and fight back. We flex our muscles, armor up our hearts, and give it a swift uppercut to the chin.

I see men do this all the time. It is the place where God-given masculine strength turns toward aggression or power. In the face of pain, men fight back and race toward addictions,[2] violence,[3] and success. Consider Cain, the father of violence. He took his pain and transformed it into a clear power-up reaction toward his brother Abel, and he committed the first murder. Jesus exposes the full extent of our disposition toward violence by naming anger as equivalent to murder. We are all guilty of powering up in some form.

Men who power up against their pain find themselves at the top of their careers and look back at the swath of destruction in their path. They can have extremely large bank accounts or extremely empty ones, depending on their emotional drug of choice. These men can be dangerous, some overtly, some subtly. Power-up men drive hard, often with a simmering anger that lies just beneath the surface. In painful moments, this anger can rise against those they love—when they are not respected by their children, when they receive their wife's disappointed look, or when they miss an opportunity at work. All of these can provoke a power-up response.

On the contrary, like a threatened tortoise, men who power down pull their heads, arms, and feet into their self-protective shells in an attempt to flee from pain. There is an internal switch that gets flipped, and they turn off, tune out, and take off. Rather than face the pain and address it head on, power-down men hope that it will silently dissipate with the passing of time. They retreat from the world into fantasy in order to numb the pain. They pull away to video games, films, sports, man caves, pornography, drinking, and the like. The popular Christian word for this is *passivity*, but powering down means so much more. It is a hollowness, an emptiness, an absence. Even with the external veneer of politeness and neighborliness, these men are emotionally vacant. It is far easier to withdraw than it is to sit in the agony of pain.[4]

Both power-up and power-down responses produce catastrophic results for men and for those around them. Richard Rohr warns us, "If we do not transform our pain, we will transmit it in some form."[5]

The experience of pain is universal. Everyone, man or woman, must face the reality of living in a painful, fractured world. That is the legacy of our Adamic line. Rohr continues,

> Pain and suffering that are not transformed are usually projected onto others, eventually distorting or destroying personal relationships, the public mood, and even total institutions and eras. One can often feel 'the pain body' in many individuals.[6]

Yet God has given us the gracious ability to *transform* our pain in order to diminish its powerful sway over our souls.

In order to face and transform our pain, we must first *identify its location, name it honestly,* and *bless it in the company of other men.*

## PAIN IDENTIFIES THE PLACE OF WOUNDING

My leg hurt. The searing pain I experienced prevented movement of any kind. I could not walk. I could not even stand up or go to the bathroom. The agony and shame of sitting on the toilet while my wife held my leg straight brings nausea even now. But the fact is, the pain was in my *leg*. Indeed, it affected the entirety of my functioning, but the white-hot sting of pain rested in my right thigh. There was no doubt where the wound was located.

The most dangerous aspect of leprosy is the loss of feeling. The nerve damage caused by this ravenous nerve-numbing disease results in nonexistent pain receptors in the extremities. In ancient times, when cooking by fires and exposure to the elements constituted a regular threat, lepers often suffered the loss of fingers, toes, and flesh because they were unaware of the location of their wound. They did not know something was wounded because they simply felt no pain.

Pain, therefore, is a gift from God. It is a nervous system response that alerts us to trouble and provides us with the necessary feedback to avoid even more catastrophic results. Emotional pain reflects physical pain.[7] As we identify the *location* of our emotional, mental, and spiritual traumas, we can begin to dress the wound and attend to our needs. As men, however, our tendency is to minimize or ignore the pain and respond instead with a power-up (fight) or power-down (flight) reflex. We go on autopilot and disregard the deeply emotional impact of the wound. Like a flashing road sign warning us of the washed-out bridge ahead, pain is an indicator that something is tragically amiss.

The fact is, all men are wounded. Pain is, unfortunately, a fact of life. But the transformation of that pain into something greater begins by identifying its location. *Where, when,* and *who* are the key questions. Where did it occur? When was the blow meted out against my heart? Who was the perpetrator of my agony? What previous parts of my story set the stage for this to be particularly painful? Rather than "blow it off" or "push through it," what might happen if we were instead to attend to the places in our stories where we have been wounded? We cannot do that unless we know where it is located.

Wounds of this nature often follow thematic storylines. The assault on the human heart does not often occur in a one-time inciting incident, but instead, it continues by repeating seemingly unrelated moments of reinforced pain. Asking the where, when, and who questions is vital to discovering the themes of your wounding. It is for this reason that knowing one's own story, with its highs and lows, with its glories and tragedies, stands as an essential element to personal, spiritual, and relational growth. Just as a doctor must first identify the wound before she can treat it, identifying our pain is the first step toward restoration.

I invite you to go back to your story timeline. Consider what you named as "T" and "t" tragedies. For many of us, it is far easier to identify the location of our "T" pain. We know what happened, when, and by whom fairly easily. However, most often, surrounding the "T's" of our lives are several unidentified "t's" we have never noticed before. For example, for the boy whose mother died, it is easier to name the "T" of her death than the "t" of his father's absence to help him navigate the devastation of the loss. Dad was busy taking care of the funeral arrangements and managing the out-of-town visitors, and he did not notice the brokenhearted little boy who had to find his own way through overwhelming grief. Or consider the boy who was abused by the neighbor. It is easier to name the pain of the abusive actions taken by a pedophile than it is to identify the pain of telling his mother what happened, but not being believed.

What pain in your story have you yet to identify?

## NAMING PAIN

Adam's first task as God's earthly ambassador was to name all the living creatures.[8] To name is to push back the curse of chaos and bring clarity and definition. By assigning a name, we set it apart, or *sanctify* it, by calling out its uniqueness and place. In the ancient Near East culture, naming a child meant providing him with an identity and a future.

For many men, however, to name the pain is equal to acknowledging its power over them. We are often resistant to giving it a name, for in so doing, we admit its effect on us. This returns us to feelings of weakness, insecurity, and not being enough. We prefer to suffer in silence than recognize what we consider our failure or frailty. However, the opposite is true. The more we name our pain, acknowledging that it not only exists but also affects us deeply, the more we create for ourselves a new path toward healing. Rohr says, "Our wounds do not become *sacred* wounds because we do not admit to having them."[9]

What, then, does naming entail? To name one's pain is simply an admission of its existence. It is not a succumbing to its power, but an acknowledgement of the wound. Many men suffer silently or unknowingly from feelings of rejection, betrayal, powerlessness, emasculation, abandonment, and shame. To name the pain is to begin to put words to the agony in such a way that says, "Yes, that actually hurt."

As I began to acknowledge and name the pain in my leg, I learned how to stop re-injuring it through my power-up stubbornness. I also stopped allowing it to push me into the crevices of despair. I saw it for what it was–a painful wound to my leg–and intentionally moved into a place of co-existence with the pain in order to heal the wound. By viewing the pain as a gift and a guide to my healing, I was able to both accept its effect on me and imagine its healing.

With emotional wounds, however, we may be fearful of blaming someone else for our pain, so we resist naming it altogether. I had no problem blaming my assailants for the wound in my leg, but when it comes to how issues of loneliness, fear, and not-enoughness entered my life, I am far more hesitant to name the pain for fear of defaming someone I love. We are often caught in a place of ambivalence, where we are torn between loyalty to a loved one and honesty about how they hurt us. To name the pain for what it is, however, is a form of honor–honor of yourself and, indeed, honor of the other.

In my counseling office, I cannot tell you how often I have heard the following defenses:

"It wasn't really *that* bad."

"I grew up in a really good home. Nothing *really* to complain about."

"My dad did his best. I can understand why he was so hard on me. He had an abusive father too."

"He didn't *mean* to hurt me. It just got out of control."

"I just pushed the limits too far for her to handle, and she snapped."

"I can't blame them. They had so much to deal with."

"I was a difficult child. I'd have done the same thing to me."

"Well, that was in the past. What can I do about it now? Better leave those things alone."

"Compared to other people's difficulties, mine are so miniscule."

"It was just fondling. At least I wasn't raped."

By minimizing the painful effect of the wound, we create increasing space for it to fester and grow. Imagine if, when I walked into the emergency room after the stabbing, the doctors and nurses had underestimated or minimized the significance of the wound and just brushed it off as a scratch. Within minutes, I would have bled out from the gurney onto the floor. By appropriately naming the wound as a *stabbing*, and seeing the extent to which my thigh had been traumatized, they were able to respond with appropriate swiftness and decisiveness.

In the same way, naming our emotional pain is a vital step toward transformation. When we shift from using vague language like "he was hard on me" to "he beat me," or from "it was weird" to "it was abuse," or from "I was a latchkey kid" to "I was neglected," we are now free to begin the journey of healing. Otherwise, we continue to live with the emotional ramifications of violence, abuse, and neglect without knowing from whence it came. As Dan Allender often says, "We cannot heal that which we have not named."[10]

First, we must identify our pain, zeroing in on where it is located, what happened, and who did it. Then, through careful reflection and consideration, we bring appropriate language to it by naming it for what it actually is. Then, and only then, can we move into the realm of blessing.

## PAIN CHART

| What We Typically Say | What It Actually *Might* Mean |
|---|---|
| My parents got divorced. | I didn't have my father/mother in the way I needed. |
| He/she touched me. It was "weird." | I was sexually abused. |
| He'd have a few beers. | My father was an alcoholic. |
| I liked to spend time alone in my room. | I felt safest in my room because of the chaos in the rest of the house. |
| My mom needed me to take care of her. | My mother used me for emotional support…a role that should have been my dad's. |
| As the oldest, I took care of my siblings. | I was the surrogate parent because our parents abdicated their responsibility. |
| His anger would get out of hand sometimes. | My father beat me. |
| I kinda discovered sex on my own. | No one guided me or taught me about what it means to be a man. |

## BLESSING THE WOUNDED PART

About 16 years after the stabbing, I returned to the scene of the incident. Though portions of our family had visited this country for various ministry reasons over the years, we had never been back as a whole. After my oldest son graduated from high school, we decided to return to show our children where they spent the earliest years of their childhood.

We visited the typical sites as tourists rather than residents, and we enjoyed the exotic wonders of the country we love. One day, we returned to the neighborhood where we raised our family and showed our awestruck children the places we frequented as we made a life abroad.

As we did so, we walked the same journey from the ferry to the apartment and traced the steps of my assault. We stopped at the bakery and stood there together on the stoop where the stabbing occurred. Though the baker who witnessed it was not there, we bought a cake and took it up the street to the park. As a family, we celebrated my life. We celebrated that my wife did not have to raise our son as a single parent or give birth to our middle daughter alone. We celebrated the life of our youngest daughter, who would not have existed had I perished that day. We celebrated the years we all had together after the stabbing and thanked God for them.

It was a hard day for me. To be there with my family and to see the wonder and gratitude in their eyes tenderized my heart in a way I did not anticipate. But even more than what it was like to be with them, the more tender place was how it was for me to be with me, the younger man who experienced the trauma. He was a good man, a bold man, a man who felt naively invincible. Standing there in the doorway of the bakery, I saw not only the moment of the stabbing, but the subsequent moments when he would sequester his heart, vacillate from rage to despair, and then learn to welcome his pain as a companion rather than a foe.

By God's grace, I was able to turn toward that man inside me and bless him. To recognize his pain and suffering, yes, but also to honor the goodness that lived within him. To speak back through the corridors of time the words he needed to hear from someone, but never had. To bring kindness to the scene of the crime and release him from his staunch commitment to keep his armor up for fear of being suddenly and surprisingly leveled once again.

We must first *identify* the pain. Where is it? What is it? Who caused it? When we reflect on the narratives of our lives, we must sink down into the actual scenes and moments of the story if we are to identify the pain. Then, we must *name* it for what it actually is. Using truthful and accurate language is crucial for us to understand the nature of our wounding. Not only was I stabbed in my body, I was stabbed in my heart. This *had* to be named in order for it to be healed. Then, and only then, can we bring kindness into the story, to *bless* the wounded parts and to honor both the validity of the pain and the one who suffered it. This is a profound journey, and one many men will never walk. Even more rare is the man who takes these steps in the community of other men.

## THE PAIN OF SUFFERING ALONE

One of the most insidious aspects of pain is its attempt to isolate. Compounded by the fear of seeming weak and needy, men often find themselves hiding their pain from other men. We have this demented notion that we must deal with it on our own.

The fact is that just as you share anatomical similarities with the other men in your Brotherhood group, you also share pain as part of your experience. Every one of you knows the sting of pain. It is as you begin to *identify, name,* and *bless* your pain...together...that you will find release and growth through it.

Men do not like to enter the pain of others. Even Jesus's closest friends slept through His moments of deepest agony.

> Then Jesus went with his disciples to a place called Gethsemane, and he said to them, "Sit here while I go over there and pray." He took Peter and the two sons of Zebedee along with him, and he began to be sorrowful and troubled. Then he said to them, "My soul is overwhelmed with sorrow to the point of death. Stay here and keep watch with me."
>
> Going a little farther, he fell with his face to the ground and prayed, "My Father, if it is possible, may this cup be taken from me. Yet not as I will, but as you will."
>
> Then he returned to his disciples and *found them sleeping*. "Could you men not keep watch with me for one hour?" he asked Peter....He went away a second time and prayed...
>
> When he came back, he again *found them sleeping*, because their eyes were heavy. So he left them and went away once more and prayed the third time...
>
> Then he returned to the disciples and said to them, "Are you still sleeping and resting? Look, the hour is near, and the Son of Man is betrayed into the hands of sinners. Rise, let us go! Here comes my betrayer!"[11]

The pain Jesus suffered in the garden was doubled by the absence of His friends. He faced the most agonizing moments of His life alone. When He needed them, they were asleep.

One of the most powerful possibilities of experiencing life together with other brothers is not the confession of sin,[12] but rather the redemption that the sharing of stories of tragedy, trauma, and pain can offer. We all long for someone to witness our lives and to understand what it was actually like to live the stories we carry. With this company of men, you now have the opportunity to transform the pain you hold, together.

When we share our stories with other men, we offer them the opportunity to identify, name, and bless our pain in ways we may never be able to on our own. They can see what we do not see. On numerous occasions when men have told their stories in a matter-of-fact way, I have watched the faces of the other men in the room. Shocked, appalled, and tearful, the responses of the listeners compel the storyteller to awaken to the significance of his wounds. To see compassion and empathy on the face of a brother, especially when he considers his story "normal," invites him to take a step back and wonder what unidentified, unnamed, and untended pain might still be there.

You need your brother to read your story with you, and he needs you to do the same.

## PERSONAL REFLECTION

- When you think about a man's experience of pain, what comes to mind?
- From the reading, what can you identify with? What is difficult to connect with?
- How do you see the church dealing with pain in men's lives?
- When you consider your own pain, do you typically power up or power down?
- How do those around you experience your pain?
- Richard Rohr says, "If we do not transform our pain, we will transmit it in some form." What do you think of his statement? How has pain been transmitted to you? How do you transmit your pain to others?
- In what ways do you find yourself minimizing your pain?
- As you shared your story in the group, what was it like for you to see and experience their responses? What were you able to identify, name, and bless in your story that you could not have without the brotherhood of men?
- What is it like for you to actually put words to the trauma you have experienced?
- As you go through this process of reflection, what do you sense God saying to you?

## GROUP DISCUSSION

- What about the topic this week was easy or difficult for you? When you think about bringing your pain to other men, what happens inside?
- What places of pain have you identified in your life?
- What is particularly raw?

- What was it like for you to experience the other men as you shared your story? What did their responses open up for you as you consider your story now?

# 9
## NEED

I can go weeks without hearing from my father. He is 79 years old, lives on his own, and drives himself every day to the skilled nursing facility where my mother sits in the final stages of Alzheimer's. For the majority of his life, he worked as a very successful attorney in downtown Denver in a firm my grandfather started. By many accounts, he was a force to be reckoned with. Even now in his older years, every doctor, nurse, or caregiver he encounters experiences his staunch commitment to avoid the appearance of need. If I do hear from him, it can only mean one of two things: either he is frustrated *I* have not called *him*, or he has finally reached a point of urgent need so great, he has exhausted all other options.

Recently, he called me at 7 a.m. on the Saturday before Thanksgiving. Without a preface, he said, "I need you to take me to urgent care."

"Okay," I replied. "Can you tell me what is going on?"

"I have a sinus infection," he said.

"How long has this been going on?" I asked.

"I don't know. Maybe a week. I need medication," he concluded.

Upon arriving at his house to pick him up, I was confronted with a man who could barely walk. He was not yet dressed, and he did not have the energy or balance to stand up from his living room chair. Tissues surrounded him, and his unkempt hair indicated he had not moved in hours. His condition was terrible.

I helped him get dressed, put on his shoes, and guided him out to my car. He coughed uncontrollably and could barely catch his breath. On the way to the nearest urgent care facility, I said, "Dad, I think you need the hospital, not urgent care. You are not good."

"No, I want urgent care. It's a sinus infection, and I just need antibiotics," he retorted in his short and punctuated manner.

Upon arriving and unloading him into a wheelchair, we waited the necessary hour to see a doctor, who took one look at him and said, "We can't treat you here. You need to go to the emergency room." I did everything I could to not let him see my massive huff and I-told-you-so eye roll, and then I commenced the process of reloading him into the car for the drive to the hospital.

In the end, he had a respiratory syncytial virus (RSV) infection coupled with pneumonia. His oxygen levels were dramatically low, and his ability to breathe was so minimal the doctors asked me for his advanced directives around end-of-life desires and intubation. He ended up staying in the hospital for five days, then was released to a rehabilitation center for a week and a half, then was moved to assisted living for a week, which was followed by two weeks of at-home physical and occupational therapy. This simple trip to urgent care turned into an eight-week journey of recovery.

And, of course, in his mind he only needed a prescription for some common antibiotics. The crazy thing is, he *still* thinks that.

As men, like my father, we are taught and conditioned to avoid the appearance of need. We are rewarded for our independence, praised for our ability to "push through the pain," and equate need with all things anti-masculine. Rather than recognize our need, we adhere to a universal vow of silence. To speak of it is to break the man code. The truth is that men don't engage need well.

It just doesn't seem "manly" to poke around in the depths of need. That is for the weak. Many men create elaborate defenses to diffuse need's power, hoping to eliminate it from ever being part of our experience. We craft more acceptable stories designed to divert attention away from our need, thereby saving face and continuing to broadcast our manliness. For some reason, for my father, a sinus infection was a far more reasonable need than pneumonia and urgent care was satisfactory since "all he needed was a pill."

For a man to admit a need, he is often viewed as less than, not strong enough, or not able to provide for himself. For a man to say, "I need ___" is to verbally admit he has a disability that impedes his participation in all things manly. To say, "I need" is to serve up your heart to another man and risk denial. Often, we find it easier to hold our needs close to our chest and only admit them when wrestled out by circumstance or stubbornness. For the most part, "Seriously, dude, get a grip. Deal with it!" echoes through our minds.

Think about it. It is a rare man who honestly speaks of his need without cowering or making light of it through sarcasm and cynicism. And I'm not talking about simple needs, like needing to borrow my neighbor's wheelbarrow for a bit of yard work (even though that can be hard). I am talking about admitting the much deeper need for other men to come alongside us, for care and tending to our hearts, and for help in areas of shame or stuckness. Need is at the core of every brotherhood, yet we rarely, if ever, admit it. The truth is, far too many men believe they need a simple antibiotic prescription when, in fact, they need the E.R.

In talking about need, what I really mean is true, heart-level need that keeps a guy up at night or drives him toward emotional hollowness or addictions. What does a man do with his need for courage when his wife is diagnosed with breast cancer? Or when he finds himself in overwhelming debt and can't pay the electric bill at the end of the month? What about the need he feels when his daughter starts to date and the shady looking guy pulls in the driveway? What about the hollowness he feels when he comes home from a long day at work and the most excited greeting he receives is from the dog? Or the constant ache of loneliness that eats away at his soul because no one truly knows what it's like to be him?

Each of these needs is real, powerful, and important. But the risk of revealing it, especially after multiple relational misfires in the past, keeps a man secluded and alone. The need is there, yet the internal oath to never speak of it again remains intact and reinforced.

On the one hand, need can be viewed as weakness; on the other hand, if a man does share a need, it may be misconstrued as an attempt at manipulation. For a guy to bring a supposed[1] need, we assume there is an angle. A classic example is how we respond to guys panhandling on the street (or maybe it's just me). Sitting there at a red light, the guy holds a cardboard sign that reads, "Anything helps." One more creative sign I recently saw said, "Girlfriend kidnapped by ninjas. Need money for ransom and Kung Fu lessons." An immediate war rages in my mind and heart. If I give this guy my spare change, what will he use it for? Will it be for shelter or food or transportation? Or will it be for booze or drugs or something worse? I immediately assume that there is some ulterior motive to his asking.

In many Christian men's settings, I see this type of manipulation happen in the form of prayer requests. A common way to close a small group is to ask the open-ended question, "How can we pray for you this week?" On several occasions, I have heard men respond with "I can't pay my rent this week; please pray for provision" or "I haven't had a date with my wife for weeks because I can't find a babysitter." While these requests may be an acknowledgment of need, they can sometimes be subtle attempts to manipulate the group to spring into action. Don't misunderstand me: I firmly believe we should help one another make it through difficult times. But there is something disingenuous when these needs are framed as prayer requests rather than actual *need*, and that just drives me mad.

For many men, this is what need is. Need = weakness. Need = angle. We do whatever we can as men to avoid these two things.

## BROTHERS AND NEEDS

One of the most famous male-male friendships in the scriptures occurred between David and Jonathan. There are a million interpretations of what their relationship entailed, but one thing is certain... how it grew.

In 1 Samuel 20:1-4, we find David convinced that King Saul desires to kill him. Like a wounded dog on the run, David finds Saul's son Jonathan and explains his perilous situation.

> Then David fled from Naioth at Ramah and went to Jonathan and asked, "What have I done? What is my crime? How have I wronged your father, that he is trying to take my life?"
>
> "Never!" Jonathan replied. "You are not going to die! Look, my father doesn't do anything, great or small, without confiding in me. Why would he hide this from me? It's not so!"
>
> But David took an oath and said, "Your father knows very well that I have found favor in your eyes, and he has said to himself, 'Jonathan must not know this or he will be grieved.' Yet as surely as the Lord lives and as you live, there is only a step between me and death."
>
> Jonathan said to David, "Whatever you want me to do, I'll do for you."[2]

David does a brave thing. Running for his life, he approaches Jonathan from a place of need. He humbles himself before Jonathan and says, "I can't do this on my own. I'm a hunted man. Will you help me?" Jonathan, an upright and trustworthy friend, agrees to help despite his suspicions and doubts. He hears and receives David's proclamation of need and responds with strength, commitment, and kindness. Throughout the remainder of the chapter, we see the friendship between these two men grow to the point that they take an oath that lasts well into future generations.[3]

The beginning of true brotherhood is a willingness to admit need. Not just tipping the hat to an accountability or men's group because it's a good idea. Not just finding help in sin management[4] or the "coulds" and "shoulds" of what it means to be a Christian man. No, it

> *The beginning of true brotherhood is a willingness to admit need.*

is a genuine recognition of the perilous journey of a man's life and the acknowledgement that we were not meant to go at it alone. Often, the first step in developing deeper male friendships is with a stagger and a limp. It is saying to the other guy, "I need you *with* me."

Several years ago, my buddy Greg Daley and I began working out together three times a week. We lived close enough to one another to make it convenient, and we had discovered enough in common to make the first moves toward a deeper friendship. After about a year (with unfortunately little progress in the muscle-building category), my schedule changed and we had to stop the workout routine, but we decided to meet once a week for coffee to keep the conversation going.

At the time I was in graduate school for counseling. Deep in my own therapeutic process, I found my conversations with Greg intellectually stimulating, like a real-life practicum of experience. I could see the theological and psychological processes at work in him, and I often slipped into "counselor mode." In reality, it was my way of self-protecting: always be the one to ask the questions and make thoughtful observations so the tables are never turned to the examination of *my* heart. It's a cool little trick. I'm sure some of you know what I mean.

One day Greg pulled the rug out from under my secure therapist's perch. He said, "I'm not going to do this. I'm not going to relate to you as a counselor only. Either you show up as *yourself* at this table and in this relationship, or we're going to have to stop. You are not my counselor. You're my friend. I'm not settling for less."[5]

Greg refused to settle for a mediocre friendship with me. In essence, he said, "I need you, and I know you need me. Admit it, or forget it." *That* was the beginning of a deeper friendship. And it all started with an acknowledgement of *need*.

Unlike King David and my friend Greg, however, men often run away from need. We have been trained to keep our needs to ourselves and to hide from one another behind well-crafted façades in order to maintain some semblance of masculine dignity. In the lofty towers of our own strength, we suffer a severe case of aloneness. We ache for another man to enter our need, yet we run from anyone who may see our vulnerability.

## WOUNDED NEED

The word "unrequited" is usually followed by the word "love," meaning love and affection that is not mutually shared. But that's not the only way the word can be used. In the area of need, many brave men have risked sharing their needs with others, only to be met with distance, disdain, or platitudes. Unrequited need could possibly be the most relationship-damaging aspect of male friendships. When a man musters up the gumption to share his need with another, but then receives blank stares and dismissal as a result, he is wounded at the point of his need. These wounds run deep, often deeper than the need itself.

Many years ago, in a conversation about need with my friend Mark, he shared how open he once was with other men about his needs. He had come to the point in his life where the relational risk of presenting a need seemed less powerful than the desire to be seen and known. But, he said, he was burned. Burned badly. Mark had been in a small group with the same men for over a year and a half. Repeatedly, after Mark shared his needs with them, he found himself distanced and alone. His needs went unrequited, and though he had spent a significant amount of time in this group, they barely remembered his name. Time after time, he found they could not handle his needs, so he retreated from the desire to share and returned into his own world of isolation and despair. The message Mark received was clear: to be a man with need meant that he was apparently not man enough. He had summoned the courage to share his need with others, and they trampled on his vulnerability. The pain of unrequited need is devastating.

## MAN ENOUGH

Where did we get the idea that "man" and "enough" belong in the same sentence? We subconsciously believe men were designed to live in isolation and complete self-sufficiency. We should not need one another, and if we do, we are somehow showing signs of being less than what we should be.

*Am I enough?*

Or more powerfully, *Am I man enough?*

What does that even mean, man enough? How does one measure a man's enoughness? Is there a scale to weigh it? Is there a yardstick or measuring tape? Is there a thermometer or speedometer? It sure would be nice.

Regardless of the measure, most men are convinced of one thing: other men are enough, but they are not. *He* has what it takes, but *I* most certainly do not. On every measure of enoughness, I know I fall to the bottom. The most likely measure of enoughness is the presence of need. Those who are most needy are obviously not enough.

In brotherhood, however, we are called to put down the scales and tape measures of one another's enoughness, especially our own, and simply acknowledge that it is a stupid idea. It just is. And while we might find it possible to stop measuring *his* enoughness, it is far more difficult to stop measuring our own. Will I ever be able to remove the "man enough" thermometer from under my own tongue?

Even in this process of brotherhood in your group, you have likely encountered an element of mutual measuring. You have made internal judgments about where you stand over and against the other men in your group. There are likely those who you think are better than you and those you rank as lower or as more needy than you. Some are smarter, some are crazier. Some are more religious, others are more pagan. Some have it together, some don't.

The reality is that need is the great equalizer of men. Every man, whether educated or not, rich or poor, famous or unknown, married or unmarried, tall or short, blue collar or white collar, needs other men. As we begin to risk the exposure of our need with each other, then we can begin to truly know the depth and importance of true brotherhood.

The moment that Greg spoke those words to me, I knew my friendship with him had shifted into something completely different–brotherhood. He reached over that table at Starbucks and yanked the tape measure from my hand. He simply said, "I don't care what your needs are. Bring it on. I can take it." That is what brothers do.

I need.

I need another man to witness my life.

I need someone else to normalize my experience, to challenge me and comfort me.

I need more than accountability. I need more than a men's breakfast or a Bible study.

I need someone to listen well to my story of trauma and tragedy.

I need a brother.

Lead with your need, because believe it or not, it opens the door to true brotherhood.

## PERSONAL REFLECTION

- How does the topic of need, as you just read it, strike you?
- What would you consider your greatest need at the moment?
- Think of a recent moment when you minimized your own need so as to not seem weak or manipulative. What happened? What was going on for you internally?
- How do you view needy men? What is your typical response to a man who admits his need? Where did you learn that perspective?
- What do you make of the friendship between David and Jonathan?
- Read 1 Samuel 18:1-4 (the beginning of their friendship).
- Then read 2 Samuel 1:25-26 (the lament of David over the death of Jonathan).
- What kinds of curiosities or questions do these two passages provoke in you?
- How do you think the men in your Brotherhood group will react to you if you admit and bring your need to them? What are your hopes? Fears?
- Most men's gatherings have an element of machismo, where guys are subconsciously trying to find their place in the pecking order of the group. How have you seen this happen in yourself during the past weeks? What would you like to change?

## GROUP DISCUSSION

- In your experience, how do men engage their need? Do they?
- In what ways would you personally like to grow in the area of naming your need to other men?

- What hesitancy do you still have in sharing your need with this brotherhood?
- How does it feel to say "I need you guys in my life" out loud to the other men?
- When you consider your own need, what would you like to acknowledge to the other men today? What are your fears as you do so?
- What would you like the others to know about your need right now?

# 10
## BLESSING

In the context of masculine relationships, we often find ourselves focusing on what is *not* right or *not* holy or *not* working. Our eyes and ears constantly search for the imperfections, both in ourselves and in others, in order to stand in judgment or offer fix-it-now solutions. We read books on improvement and growth, and our spiritual to-do lists often include the four-letter word "more." More prayer. More Bible study. More spiritual leadership of my family. More service. More giving. More evangelism. More. More. More. And the more I compare myself to the other guy, the more I discover I lack.[1]

In the end, "more" is not helpful. Yes, we need to be pursuing growth and maturity. And yes, we need to be attentive to the ways we engage that are stagnant, empty, and harmful. But far too often, unbeknownst to us, we fall into a pattern of *second-story management* rather than *first-story pursuit*. In our contending with our loss of innocence and our woundedness and pain from the traumas and tragedies of our lives, we do our damndest to push back the curse and gain access to Eden. So much of our lives is spent in an attempt to unwrite the story we don't want to live without remembering, as C.S. Lewis says, "there is a magic [story] deeper still."[2]

The man you were designed to be has very little to do with *you*. It has far more to do with God and the likeness of His image *in you*. When you consider a reflection, the importance is placed not on the mirror itself, but on the One being reflected. It takes someone other than the mirror to *identify, name,* and *bless* the glorious manifestation of God in you. In order for your character to be seen and recognized, you need other men to peer deeply into your soul and exclaim, "I see Him in you!"

Through this process, you have taken the bold step to invite other men into the holy sanctuary of your story. For many men, this has been the first experience of vulnerably and honestly opening up their lives to other guys. So many men's groups focus on the failures, the sins, the places where "more" is needed to correct and corral the waywardness of your soul. But here, as these brothers have tread upon long-forgotten territory with eyes attuned to the divine poetry originally written into your life, they have come to know the face of the Master as they have witnessed His masterpiece in you.

From a long and hard life on the streets of Calcutta, Mother Teresa spoke wise words with regard to the human condition. She said, "I have come to realize more and more that the greatest disease and the greatest suffering is to be unwanted, unloved, uncared for, to be shunned by everybody, to be just nobody."[3] In essence, the greatest of human pain comes when the dignity of our souls, emblazoned by God, remains unseen and unnoticed. It is only when we turn toward one another in godly reverence and mysterious wonder that we see His fingerprint.

The fact is, we are all too familiar with our failings. Rarely do we need someone else to point them out. We know the areas of our lives that need attention. One of the greatest gifts brothers are meant to offer one another is an honest reflection not of failing, sin, and shadow, but of glory. Yet we shy away from this deeply manly gift because it has been so woefully neutered by both society and the church. To look into the eyes of a brother and to name that which is good feels both awkward and wrong. It is the longing of every man's heart, yet we balk at it for fear our words will be misunderstood or mistaken.

Men just don't talk like that with other men.

To speak of another man's glory, we must be willing to step into unknown territory—his heart. This feels both thrilling and dangerous. This risk requires that we peer into his soul without violating or assuming. Instead, we must get to know him, spend time with him, see him for who he really is, and come to know and honor his stories. We must come to know his character and build bridges of trust in order to have the right to speak.

And we are desperate for men to speak words of blessing to us and over us, for words are a man's primary means of bringing forth life in the world.

I believe both men and women are called to partner with God as co-creators on earth. We are meant to collaborate with Him in the bringing forth of life. And while all of humankind shares this calling, the essence of that partnership manifests differently for men and women.

Come into my home, and you will see my wife's life-giving nature. Everywhere she goes, she creates beauty and goodness. From the decor of our house to the aromas of the candles she burns or the food she crafts, you experience the goodness of God through the hands and presence of my wife. Almost everything she touches turns to gold. As for our children, she first gave them her body in ways I cannot even fathom. From the moment of her first period as her young body prepared to someday weave life, to the worried and sleepless nights of our children's teenage years, she has sacrificed herself in the service of their well-being. From the co-labor of her womb and breasts, she has sprung and sustained life in ways that will be forever impossible for me. The life my wife brings to the world is through the offering of herself physically, emotionally, creatively, and spiritually. She has created everything from little humans to anti-trafficking organizations, from stunning art to renovated homes.

This is not the case for me. My contribution to the creation of our children involved a single cell, and my body did not endure the long suffering of periods, pregnancy, or birth as hers did. While I have stood watch over her labors, whether in the delivery room with our children or on our long walks as she labors for their goodness and well-being in the world, the essence of my co-creation with God to bring forth life is of a completely different nature.

Just as women have a unique way they partner with God to bring life in the world, so too do men. Every man has the potential to bring life to others through the power and substance of his words.

Consider the wisdom of Solomon recorded for us in the book of Proverbs:

> The tongue has the power of life and death, and those who love it will eat its fruit.[4]
>
> Gracious words are a honeycomb, sweet to the soul and healing to the bones.[5]
>
> The words of the reckless pierce like swords, but the tongue of the wise brings healing.[6]
>
> The words of a man's mouth are deep waters; the wellspring of wisdom is a flowing brook.[7]

I believe words of blessing are the life-giving womb of men. Just as God *spoke* the world into existence, there is immense generative power in a man's words. We were born into this world looking for and longing for the kind of words that speak life to our questioning, withering, and dead places. As the wise sage of Proverbs tells us, words are like honeycomb to the soul, water to the heart, and healing to the body. We all need the sustenance of these types of words.

Reflect on your life, and consider the times when you received life-giving words from another man. Maybe it was your father, your uncle, your coach, your older brother, your grandfather, or your youth leader. You may have anticipated them, but most likely they came at a moment and in a way that caught you off guard. Your heart likely struggled to receive them. These words brought life, and though we may have received them somewhere in our life's journey, most of us are painfully aware of how rare they have been.

Likewise, as Proverbs and other scriptures warn, words can be equally dangerous. The tongue can both give life and destroy it, bolster the heart or pierce it. Harsh words stir up anger,[8] and absent words leave behind a vacuous wasteland. Our words have power, especially for those with whom we have journeyed to the deepest places in our lives and stories.

*Men, the world needs your life-giving words of blessing.*

Men, the world needs your life-giving words of blessing.

I believe in every man's heart God crafted a nuclear power plant of words. When functioning well, that plant provides light and warmth to many. From him flows a masculine substance by which life and goodness grow. When a man partners with God to co-create life through the provision of his words, the world both grows and finds rest. A man with words of blessing lights up his community, energizes his world, and offers warm protection from the darkness and cold.

But if that man's internal nuclear power plant is not functioning, where the switch is turned off and its production of life-giving words is missing, those around him experience emptiness, darkness, and a frostbitten cold. Like the vacuum of space where no air, breath, or sound exists, the wordless man suffocates and freezes everyone around.

Likewise, if the plant inside a man cracks, if containment is broken and the unbridled and unguided nuclear power begins to ooze, his words become toxic and dangerous for all around. With a violence many of us know all too well, they destroy the heart and decimate the soul. Where life and goodness should exist, those around this man know only the sharp edge of his words. Rather than giving life, they mete out death.

Take a moment now to peer through the annals of time. Where have you known the life-destroying power of a man's words? Maybe they were absent, leaving you wondering and questioning and confused. Maybe a few words existed, but only a few, and you were forced to feast on the table scraps of the meager offerings he made. Or maybe you know well the harshness of violent and cutting words, designed to destroy and emasculate your heart. These are the words that sealed the second story's power over you and convinced you that goodness and divine poetry were never written on your heart in the first place.

My friends, the words of a man are his ultimate superpower. There are no neutral words. As my brother Bart Lillie says, "Blessing is the native tongue of the first story."

I am sure by now you are taking stock of your own life as a man, reviewing how you have engaged the reality of the nuclear power plant in your heart. Where have you brought light and life? Where have you withheld your words and abandoned those most desperate to hear from you? How have you used your words as a weapon, severing hope and destroying dreams? It is sobering to review ourselves in light of our superpower. And Uncle Ben in *Spiderman* famously said, "With great power comes great responsibility."[9]

Jesus Himself received the verbal blessing of the Father. Before launching into His life of ministry, He accepted God's words to cover Him, call Him, and remind Him who He was. In Matthew 3:16-17, we read,

As soon as Jesus was baptized, he went up out of the water. At that moment heaven was opened, and he saw the Spirit of God descending like a dove and alighting on him. And a voice from heaven said, "This is my Son, whom I love; with him I am well pleased."[10]

There, before the crowds and in sight of all the people, God opened the heavens and offered His son His words of recognition, care, and pleasure. How many of us long for these exact words to be spoken over us? I dare say, everyone.

As such, to conclude this season of your brotherhood, after all men have had the opportunity to share their stories and be seen and known, I invite you to experience the life-giving power of words. God has granted this superpower to you and every man in your group. Think about it: you are equally endowed with the capacity to offer words of blessing. They are wanted and needed, but all too often left unattended and unintended. Therefore, I invite you to blessing.

## HOW TO BLESS

Blessing is a foreign concept in our Western world. Many of us know we need *something*, some sort of soul-level nourishment that, like a hearty meal, will fill us up and bring us life. But we have no idea how to offer or receive blessing.

Blessing is different from encouragement. The word "courage" stems from the French word *couer*, or "heart." To have courage, therefore, is to have an internal strength or bravery in the face of difficulty. Encourage, then, refers to the process of "giving heart" and is usually used situationally, as when a man is about to ask a woman to marry him, when he is about to go bungee jumping, or as he heads to an important interview. At those times, a man needs encouragement.

You can encourage a person you don't even know. Maybe you've just met someone on the metro or at the grocery store, and in some way you have an *I - Thou* encounter with him. You've become aware, curious, and kind as he shares with you snippets of his life or struggles. Despite the brevity of your relationship, you can offer him words of encouragement as he faces his challenges.

Certainly, for those closer to us, these words are important as well. We need to freely offer encouragement to our wives, children, friends, and coworkers. Whether it is before our son's first freshman football game or our wife's appointment with the doctor, "giving heart" in moments like these makes all the difference. These are good and holy and important words, but this is not a blessing.

Blessing is not situationally driven, but it serves more as a *covering* or a *digestion* of life and purpose. To bless someone means to speak words of insight, impact, and consecration over him in order to sanctify or bestow favor. In this way, a blessing is both a celebration and recognition of the past (both good and bad) and a prophecy of the future as it is said now in the present. A blessing holds the tension of the now and the not yet. As a recognition of the past, present, and future, it stands as both a mourning of what has been and a celebration and calling of what will yet be. In a way, blessing acknowledges the difficult road traveled thus far and plows the way toward a better tomorrow.

Consider this: while encouragement offers much needed fuel for the journey ahead by giving heart and hope for challenging circumstances, blessing lays a mantle upon the shoulders of the recipient, giving identity and purpose.

In order to offer a blessing, we must be aware of the deeper story of a person's life. We have entered the realms of his second story with him, identifying and naming his wounds and his pain. We have listened generously and intently to his false narratives, all the while searching for the glimmer of his first story to shine out from beneath the ashes. To offer words of blessing is to speak life into his first story once again. It is to say, "I know the pain and struggles you have endured so far on this journey, but I see a man who ___. Your tragedies have wounded you, yes, but I see beyond them to the divine masterpiece in you."

This kind of man-to-man engagement is foreign to most of us. We just don't speak to one another in these ways. When we first launched Restoration Project and started including verbal public blessings into the architecture of every experience, men often pushed back and resisted. For many, it was just too new, too odd, or too embarrassing. Men would say, "I don't know how to do this!" or "What if I mess it up?" The truth is, just as one learns how to ride a bicycle or cast a fly rod, so too can we learn how to speak these kinds of words over one another.

Here is what I'm boldly proposing: at the next gathering of your Brotherhood, be extra intentional about creating a space where you can verbally bless one another. That means, do not meet in a cafe or brewhouse. It means establishing firm boundaries so your kids don't come barreling into the basement. Set aside a good amount of time, and prepare yourselves according to the following suggestions:

- In your journal, write down the name of each man in your group. Then, prayerfully reflect on the stories he has shared throughout the duration of your Brotherhood. Ask God to show you the first story in him while also recognizing and remembering the second. What do you notice of the divine in him? What masterpiece of God's goodness have you caught glimpses of along the way? What glory is he too afraid to believe is true about him? Make several notes about each guy.
- Then, start to write your thoughts. Some words are better than no words, so just start writing. It does not need to be poetic or overly articulate, but make sure it is true to your heart for that man. If you were in his shoes, what would you be desperate to hear from other men? What might you be terrified to hear? What do you love about him?

- Write it down, let it sit for a day or two, and then come back to it with fresh and prayerful eyes.
- On the day of your gathering, be prepared to speak your blessing over each man in front of the whole group. Yes, there is power in the words alone, but when they are witnessed by other men, their power increases.
- I recommend one man is randomly selected to occupy the "hot seat," while everyone else takes turns to offer him their blessing. Some groups choose to have one person act as a "scribe," capturing the blessings in written form to be reflected on in the future. Other groups choose to write their blessings on notecards, read them aloud, and then give them to the man at the end.
- When speaking the blessing, I have found it helpful to stand and face each other in the middle of the group. If both men are comfortable, the one offering the blessing may reach out and put his hand(s) on the shoulder of the receiving person. This communicates connectedness and care and offers a level of strong tenderness between you.
- After each man offers his blessing, our tradition at Restoration Project is to corporately say, "So say we all!" This seals the words in collective agreement that the words spoken are good and true.
- As you receive the blessings, the only requirements of you are to stay present, listen attentively and without argument, and to simply respond with, "Thank you."
- Once all blessings are offered to the man in the hot seat, he then chooses the next man to be the blessing recipient.

There is something deeply important in the ceremonial nature of a blessing time such as this. Just as the sharing of stories is holy and sacred work, so too is the power of blessing. Receiving heartfelt words spoken by honest and trustworthy men is an experience like none other. Often, cheers and glasses are raised in unison, and tears of tenderness fall amongst brothers. It is truly otherworldly.

It is my deep hope to rally a generation of men who purposefully and regularly engage opportunities to co-labor with God to bring life and healing to the world through substantial words of blessing. Experience it, and you will never be the same. And once you experience it, you will look for ways to create space for blessing again, and again, and again. If there is a God-honoring addiction for men, it is an addiction to offering words of blessing to the world around him. Start and practice with your brothers, then move to your wives, children, churches, and communities. In doing so, your nuclear power plant of blessing will soon light up the world.

## PERSONAL REFLECTION

- Up until now, what has the word blessing meant to you?
- Consider a moment in which you experienced words of blessing from another man. How was that for you? What happened inside of you? How did that shape you?
- Think of a time when you needed words of blessing, but either received a curse or nothing at all. What happened in your inner world at that moment? What was the fallout?
- How do you think the other men are feeling about offering blessing to the group?
- How are you feeling about blessing the other men in your Brotherhood group?
- How are you feeling about receiving blessing?
- Giving or receiving–which is more difficult for you?
- Take a few moments to think about each man and pray for him. Write down words that you feel God has for him. What do you think he needs to hear from other men?

## GROUP DISCUSSION

There are no discussion questions this week. Take the risk. One at a time, bless each other as is outlined in the chapter.

# EPILOGUE: WHAT'S NEXT?

The challenge you now face is the continuation of your brotherhood. When men are given structure and task, they often rise to the occasion and succeed beyond expectation. But when that structure is removed, when the book comes to an end, or when the credits roll, men often find themselves standing alone in the dark alone once again. I know this all too well, and I have struggled for years to maintain a connection with a brotherhood of men. At times, it has been deep and rich and life-giving; at other times, I have been tempted to throw up my hands at the enormity of the task.

One of the great challenges of writing *anything* is the expectation for you to live out what you have written. Indeed, it is much easier to say or write these things than it is to live them. The reality is none of us lives out brotherhood consistently well. In many cases, we ascend and descend the ladder of masculine relationship, moving in seasons toward brotherhood or away. I know this is true of me. Yet one thing remains constant—the desire and need to be in an intentional community with other men.

There are times when we need to say goodbye to some men and

hello to others. There are moments when we must acknowledge, whether for specific individuals or for a group as a whole, we have come to a crossroads, and, out of love and honor, we must transition into a different form of engagement with one another. Good endings are just as important as good beginnings.[1]

But regardless of our so-called "success" in the brotherhood arena, the road onward must continually be a longing for more, a striving toward deeper relationships, and a commitment to hope. Only then will we begin to see change. The truth still remains: *men become men through other men, and it is our task to keep each other living as men.*

It has been my task to "prime" the pump for brotherhood to occur in your midst. I have endeavored to give you categories to consider and questions to answer, yet no matter how hard I try, the onus is on you to pursue your brotherhood further. The choice is yours.

## THE ELUSIVENESS OF BROTHERHOOD

You may not feel any closer to understanding manhood, masculinity, or even brotherhood. The quest remains. However, the best place for you to learn about these things is not in a book or a study or a class. The most life-transforming place for you to grow and mature in these areas will always be in the company of other men. From the beginning, God created us to be relational and connected people, and the call of the gospel has always been unto *withness*. Pursue that, and you will find your heart and life drawn toward God. You may have heard the adage, "We become like the people we are around." I believe it is true; therefore, the quest for brotherhood is one of the most important tasks of your life.

You have had the opportunity to experience something new, something different. You have stepped into the sacred landscape of your own story and the stories of others. You have listened to one another's stories and heard about one another's journeys through life. You have learned how to create an experiential space where the souls of men can be more easily explored. You have said no to masculine mediocrity while embracing something far deeper and riskier for your male relationships. You have hunted for each other's glory, the divinely poetic masterpiece written into your souls before the beginning of time. You have blessed one another, offering words of life, vision, and hope drawn from the masculine energy within you. My prayer is that this has been a rich and trajectory-altering experience with one another.

If you have come one centimeter closer to experiencing brotherhood with other men, then this exercise has been monumentally successful. The challenge now is to continue to take it one step deeper, one step closer, and one step higher.

Brotherhood, in the end, is participation. It is a choice to be involved in other men's lives in ways our society diminishes. The result, therefore, is intangible and ever-evolving. No one can place a finger or put a value on true brotherhood. The reality is, however, everyone can identify those places where brotherhood does *not* exist. My hope is that you have come to a place in the midst of your gathering where you have tasted what true brotherhood is and can be, and that you persevere with intention and longing.

> *Brotherhood exists when men honor one another both for who they have been as men, but far more for who they are becoming.*

## KEYS TO BROTHERHOOD

If I were to summarize the essential elements of true brotherhood, the following statements might come close:

- Brotherhood exists when men choose to stand together, boldly confronting our modern conceptions of male-male relationships by intentionally and emphatically inviting one another to something deeper.
- Brotherhood exists when men navigate the relational altitude, being willing to dive down below the typical 30,000-foot level of masculine engagement to the ground level of the heart at any given moment.
- Brotherhood exists when we acknowledge our need for other men and step into the pain our lives have held, bringing awareness, curiosity, and kindness into the particularities of our stories where wounding and tragedy occurred.
- Brotherhood exists when glory stands as the bastion of hope, where men boldly and honestly look into one another's souls, piercing through the false narrative of the second story, seeking to find the reflection of the King, and then reminding one another of their first story.
- Brotherhood exists when the sterility and domesticity of modern life is pushed back, and space is created for men to experience rawness, ruggedness, risk, and wildness in one another's presence. This will look different for every brotherhood. Given the context and the individual men's preferences and personalities, men need to find spaces where their hearts can be unfettered and free.
- Brotherhood exists when stories are both read and written, when men can peer into one another's lives and find meaning, purpose, and direction together. Brothers grow when the vulnerable and sacred space of story is opened and honored.
- Brotherhood exists when men stand together in the midst of life's storms, picking one another up after being thrown down. Together, they pursue God's heart and

calling toward maturity in the midst of trial and suffering.
- Brotherhood exists when men honor one another both for who they have been as men, but far more for who they are becoming.
- Brotherhood exists between *men*. Plain and simple.

## CALL OF BROTHERHOOD

It is up to you. Where you will take what you have experienced now rests fully in your hands. You have the opportunity to go one of three ways. First, you can thank the men for what you have seen, heard, and done. You can give them a high five and bless them on their journey. You can simply say goodbye.

Second, you can prayerfully identify a few men with whom you have connected more deeply. As you review your experience, there may be some men who stand out as possible lifelong comrades. For whatever reason, you found a common language or wavelength on which to connect. From here, you can choose to allow them to fall by the wayside, or you can choose to initiate further to see what may result.

Or third, you may choose to continue this Brotherhood, recognizing and honoring one another as vastly different yet remarkably similar men. Some may opt out for their own reasons. Some may not be able to commit. But there are likely some who will want to continue the rhythm of gathering for the sake of journeying together.

Regardless of what you now choose, it is my prayer that the ache for authentic masculine friendships has been somehow touched, fed, and fanned into flame, and that you will become more than a man. I pray that you will become a part of a lifelong brotherhood.

## SUGGESTIONS FOR NEXT STEPS

Through the years, many Brotherhood groups have requested additional content and material to dive into together. To this, let me share a few thoughts.

First, the greatest and most important text for any group is not the book, video, or even scripture you are studying. The most life-transforming text you can read is the text of *your story*. Therefore, whatever centerpiece you choose to put in the middle of your Brotherhood table, I urge you to keep your stories front and center. This means always coming back to the deeper investigation of your story. The content of our stories can never fully be explored.

As an example, one creative Brotherhood chose several prompts, such as "courage," "disappointment," "father," "renewed hope," and so on. Then, they each wrote and read a story from their lives related to that prompt in their group, engaging one another from the key postures of awareness, curiosity, and kindness. They mutually pursued each man's first story while sharing hours of both tears and laughter around the fire. *This* is brotherhood. There is no end to content when you consider the breadth, depth, and complexity of our lives.

For those groups who enjoy having some thought-provoking meat to chew together, I invite you to read my book, *Sage: A Man's Guide Into His Second Passage*. Here, I unpack a host of additional material and invite men to consider the first half of their lives, what it has entailed, where they might be stuck, and what they need to do in order to make the intentional movement into the second half. I also explore categories of the sage, what I believe to be the pinnacle of the masculine journey on this earth. At the end of every chapter are questions that may be helpful to discuss as a group. Yet again, the greatest content to bring to your group are not my thoughts or even yours, but your story. The introduction for *Sage* is at the end of this book for you to preview.

I also invite you to consider participating in the plethora of experiences and resources Restoration Project provides men for the deeper masculine journey. Join us on a backpacking adventure, where we facilitate intentional investigations of your story. Or bring your son or daughter on a fathering expedition specifically designed to deepen your relationship and grow them into world citizens. You can find all of these opportunities at www.restorationproject.net/experiences.

Additionally, when we pause long enough to reflect on the narratives of our lives, we may find we need additional help to navigate through the tragedies and traumas we find buried there. Seeking help from a trained story sherpa is one of the most courageous and masculine actions a man can take. If at any point you find yourself here, I invite you to reach out to my team of excellent story practitioners at ReStory Counseling (www.restory.life). Regardless of where you are in the world, our team is equipped to provide you with the care you need and deserve.

And finally, in overwhelming gratitude for the honor you have given me to read my words and engage this journey, I want to offer you a gift. I have created an online course called the *ReStory Course,* which is designed for people who desire further training and awareness of how to engage their stories. It is an at-your-own-pace video series with a companion workbook. This may also provide your group several deepening prompts for engagement. Use the code "BROTHERHOOD" for a discount at checkout. Find the course here: www.restory.life/restory-course

I hearken back to the Apostle Paul, who encourages us to live into what we *have* rather than what we lack. In Philippians 3:16 he says, "Only let us live up to what we have already attained."[2] What we have already attained. *Already*. Regardless of size, experience, or expertise, in each of us men there is an already-ness that has occurred. Yes, there is a hope for more, but inherent in His work in us, we are already something. Already.

> *"Not that I have already obtained all this,
> or have already arrived at my goal,
> but I press on to take hold of that
> for which Christ Jesus took hold of me."*
> Philippians 3:12

## PERSONAL REFLECTION

- As *Brotherhood Primer* comes to an end, spend some significant time reflecting on what you have *experienced* more than what you have learned.
- How has this experience been the same or different from other groups in which you have participated?
- What are some key highlights of your experience that you would like to remember?
- In what ways did this experience not meet your hopes or expectations? Do you have any sense of why?
- In your opinion, how would you state the difference between being a brother versus being part of a brotherhood?
- Ask the Lord to lead you as you reflect over the last several weeks. What does He still want you to learn or experience?
- Why is it so hard for men to be in meaningful relationships with one another?
- Why is it hard for *you* to be in relationship with other men?
- If you could do this over, what would you do differently?
- How have you seen yourself move toward acting more like a brother to the men in the group?
- How would you like to move into even deeper places of brotherhood after this is over?

## GROUP DISCUSSION

- This is your last experience together in the primer. Naturally, it is my hope that your Brotherhood group will continue for many seasons to come. Today, spend time together reflecting on your first few conversations. Then recall together key moments when the atmosphere in your group shifted and new things began to happen.
- When did this gathering of men become a brotherhood?
- What are some of the most significant moments for each of you through the duration of this experience?
- What are some celebrations?
- What are some sorrows?
- Essential to brotherhood is honest communications. As you read the final chapter and considered the future of this group, what were your thoughts and desires? Do you want to continue? Do you want to end?
- How will each of you incorporate this experience into your lives?
- Spend some time honoring one another by sharing how you have experienced manhood differently because of the men in this group. "Men become men through other men." How has this happened for you in this brotherhood?
- What have you seen in others that is deeply masculine?
- When you think of the future for the other guys, what do you see?
- How have you been changed by your experience of these men, generally and specifically?
- Why does the world need these men?
- What is your hope on their behalf?
- Pray for each other.

# NOTES

## 1. PREPARATION: WHAT I'M TALKING ABOUT

1. John Eldredge first began using the word "heart" in reference to men with his book *Wild at Heart,* published in 2001. While John's message has helped thousands of men reclaim what was lost, others still have a difficult time connecting with the *heart* language. It's okay. Call it what you will, it's that inner part of you that experiences longing.
2. The 2009 movie *I Love You, Man* is a funny (yet R rated) story of a friendless man looking for a best man for his wedding. Awkwardness and man-dates abound. Don't watch this on a man-date. It would be weird.
3. I refer to several of these films during the *Man Maker Project* "Man Year," helping dads have intentional conversations with their sons about what it means to become a man.
4. It's now been 27 years!
5. Gregory Boyle, *Tattoos on the Heart: The Power of Boundless Compassion* (New York: Free Press, 2010), 14.
6. In Hebrew: *'ach.* In Greek: *adelphos.* The variety of meanings are far too numerous to indicate here. Look it up, and you'll be amazed. It is from this root for brother and the word for *love* that we get the name "Philadelphia," meaning "the city of brotherly love."
7. Yet everything in our culture seeks to isolate men from one another. Yes, there may be things we do together or in one another's presence, but the notion of true togetherness is rare. Consider how technology has pushed men to pseudo-connection, or even how televised sports removes connection and makes the activity the point. I have nothing against sitting and watching the game together, but this cannot be the sole point of contact between men. There *has* to be more.
8. John 15:15, New International Version.
9. William M. Struthers, *Wired for Intimacy: How Pornography Hijacks the Male Brain* (Downers Grove, IL: InterVarsity Press, 2009).
10. I give a range here because some groups may need longer for some of the sections.
11. Please note that some of our beta-groups have attempted to double up and do two weeks' worth of content in one longer evening. This failed miserably, mostly because this primer is not about the content, but about the relationships built. You can't rush brotherhood. I strongly suggest that you block 10 to 16 weeks on the calendar. Due to time constraints, some guys may not be able to meet *every* week, but do your best to get some time on the calendar, *roughly* a week apart. The more you can stick to the rhythm of regularity, the better it goes.

## 2. MANHOOD

1. Recently, as I drove my family up into the Rocky Mountains for a Father's Day hike, we passed hundreds of men in waders as they fly-fished in the middle of the Big Thompson River. I commented to my wife, "I'd like to try that someday." She responded, "Why? So you can feel like a man?" I answered, "In fact, yes. Maybe they've found the secret."
2. Though this has indeed been the case in the past, it is anti-biblical.
3. I believe God doesn't make mistakes. There is no "whoops!" with God, no accidental brush stroke in his divine artistry. Even the tiniest portion of creation is delightfully intended. And yes, every part of that creation is fractured and broken as a result of humanity's willful disconnection from God and subsequent exile from Eden. But God's intention is not subject to the fall because it exists within God himself and before time began.
4. Abigail Favale, *The Genesis of Gender: A Christian Theory* (San Francisco: Ignatius Press, 2022), 123-124.
5. Favale gives space for the brokenness of the world and recognizes the many sexual disorders that can occur in the reproductive process, such as boys being born without a penis or girls born without a fully formed vagina, etc. This is why she uses language with regard to the body's reproductive organization around gamete production. I encourage you to read her book.
6. I am aware of the line in the sand I am drawing here. And I am also aware that many who read this will be confused and potentially offended. Some may wonder about their own sexuality, orientation, or gender identity. I can guarantee you, many readers will have children who are wondering about these things themselves. It is not my aim to ostracize, demean, harm, or diminish anyone in this discussion. And, as I have said, I need some theological anchor to tether my own understanding for myself. That is what this is. Keep reading for more explanation of my theological understanding. I speak here as an ordained Christian minister informed by the scriptures, not as a therapist or counselor.
7. In one of the initial *Brotherhood Primer* groups, one man could not stay in the room during the discussion of this chapter.
8. Obviously, more broadly, it's your reproductive organization. But if penises are hard to talk about, then gamete production is even worse.
9. I am actually working on something I'm calling "A Theology of the Penis." Stay tuned.
10. Gen. 1:26-27, NIV; italics added.
11. Eros = erotic love; Philia = brotherly love or friendship; Storge = affectionate love; Agape = unconditional love; Mania = lustful or obsessive love (not necessarily real "love" at all)
12. Throughout ancient history, this was a well-known practice for rulers and kings. They would have statues carved "in their likeness" and placed at strategic places throughout the far reaches of their kingdoms so people would know on whose land they tread. Additionally, kings with expansive kingdoms would send ambassadorial regents to various districts in order to rule in the king's stead. These men would have the authority and power of the king himself. This practice continued

for millennia, and we see it thousands of years later in a confrontation between Pontius Pilate and Jesus, a fascinating reversal of God's initial intent.
13. A quick Google search for "zakar" retrieves a wealth of knowledge on the word, but I would not recommend it. As you can imagine, an overwhelming number of disturbing images fill the screen. Keep in mind, the internet is a deeply fallen place.
14. For those who may be interested, my friend Christy Bauman wrote an fascinating book, *The Theology of the Womb*, in which she investigates how the female body uniquely evidences the character of God.
15. Ps. 62:11-12, NIV.
16. I will return to this concept in a future chapter when we discuss the power of kindness.
17. Phil. 1:6.
18. And girls too. Boys, girls, and wives lost their men to the tyranny of work. Unintentionally stepping out of their fathering roles, many men dove head-long into the singular role of "provider," effectively losing contact with their families. And while both men and women worked hard to make this country what it is, the country lost one of its most necessary assets—men engaged and present in the lives of others. Generations of men were lost, and we are paying the price to this day.
19. I have written extensively about the process of raising a boy into a man through an intentional rite of passage process. Check out *Man Maker Project: A Father's Guide to Initiating His Son to Manhood*. Additionally, I invite you to Restoration Project's multitude of fathering experiences designed to deepen your relationship with your son or daughter. Visit www.restorationproject.net for details.
20. I do believe that discipline and purpose are vastly important in the lives of men. Too often men succumb to the mind-numbing state of passivity and avoidance. However, while *action* is a godly quality, it does not gain or win manhood. It merely refines it.

## 3. BROTHERHOOD

1. See my other book, *Man Maker Project: A Father's Guide to Initiating His Son to Manhood*, for more of what I mean here.
2. Gen. 2:9, NIV.
3. NIV.
4. I.C.E. stands for "In Case of Emergency." First responders often look for emergency contacts in people's phones using this acronym.
5. Obviously, in adoption situations, DNA is not shared, but the parents are still the ones to make the brotherly decisions.
6. In this situation, it was not only his brothers, but his parents as well. And yet, had the brothers, even *one* brother, turned toward him with the determination to bless, his lifelong struggle with relational attachment would have had a vastly different outcome.
7. I have seen many siblings of mentally disabled people, especially brothers, turn away from their needy family members—brother by blood, but distant acquaintance by choice. The shame and burden is often too much to bear.
8. If you can remember Big Wheels and Green Machines, I toast you. You should read *Sage*.

9. That neighborhood bully got what was coming to him. Years later, at about 11 p.m., several squad cars ripped up our normally peaceful cul-de-sac and burst through the front door of his family's house, only to lead him away in handcuffs. Haven't heard from him since.
10. "-*hood*" search on dictionary.com

## 4. SPACE

1. Pet peeve: why is it that the account of Noah has been turned into a zoological feel-good story? Yes, two-by-two the animals came. But we forget that death and drowning occurred outside the window of Noah's safe ocean liner. It is a tragedy, not a barnyard comedy. Oh, that gets me.
2. NIV.
3. NIV.
4. NIV.
5. I attribute this language to John Eldredge and his great work, *Wild at Heart*.
6. This is often a criticism of Eldredge's perspective. Many men who do not share his love for the outdoors find it difficult to engage with his writing. John talks of stalking an elk in the high country as an expression of masculinity. From my understanding, John is not saying that all men must have this gritty outdoor passion, but rather that all men have a heart-level engagement gauge that is squelched by sterility.
7. Why is it that Christians are so unable to obey the fourth commandment? Why do we take murder more seriously than Sabbath? We teach our children not to say "Oh my God!" in observance of the third commandment, and to "Honor your father and mother" in observance of the fifth, but we are woefully negligent in teaching them to rest, play, and delight in the holiness of Shabbat.
8. Lev. 11:44-45, 19:2 and 20:7, 26 and 1 Pet. 1:13-16.
9. NIV.
10. There is far too much with regard to the dwelling of God among men to adequately address here. In summary, in Eden, the fullness of God dwelt with humanity. God, Adam, and Eve played together without separation, but with the entry of sin, the cosmic rift between God and man broke the serenity of full togetherness. It is remarkable, then, that the Apostle John gives us a glimpse of the complete removal of this rift when once again "the dwelling of God is among men" (Rev. 21:3).
11. Acts 17:24, NIV.
12. Interestingly, *zakar* has another secondary meaning: "The one who remembers." Food for thought.
13. Heb. 10:25, NIV.
14. Not sure if you've ever done this, but google "Google office" for some fun pictures of how they create an environment of fun in the midst of productivity.
15. Wendell Berry, *Given: New Poems* (Washington, DC: Shoemaker & Hoard, 2005).
16. https://www.sherithisrael.org/news.html?post_id=154650
17. And who doesn't like to pee outside on a freezing cold December eve?!
18. I once facilitated a men's retreat close to a lake. The camp offered canoes and kayaks for our men to use. However, in order to venture out on the lake, each man had to wear a life jacket (mostly sized for Girl Scouts), and we had to have a life-

guard (who, no fault of her own, was a high school sophomore—no match for the ±200 lb. men whose lives she was to guard) on the beach. Needless to say, no man ventured out on the lake.
19. In what universe would a "gentleman" ever find himself in a place designed to treat women as objects of unbridled lust?
20. In light of what I just wrote, you can now more deeply understand the disdain I have for the shallowness of most confessional men's groups. There is so much more to a man's heart than his sin. We have often said, "The landscape of a man's heart is a holy place." We must treat the space between two men as sacred.

## 5. WHAT IS YOUR STORY? PART I

1. Daniel Taylor, *The Healing Power of Stories: Creating Yourself Through the Stories of Your Life* (New York, NY: Doubleday, 1996), 6. This work is a fantastic and accessible entry into the notion of story. I highly recommend it.
2. I highly recommend Viktor Frankl's book, *Man's Search for Meaning*, as well as Parker Palmer's work titled *Let Your Life Speak*.
3. Dan Allender, *To Be Told: God Invites You to Coauthor Your Future* (Colorado Springs, CO: WaterBrook Press, 2005), 3.
4. John O'Donohue,. interview by Krista Tippett, *On Being*, podcast audio, February 28, 2008. https://onbeing.org/programs/john-odonohue-the-inner-landscape-of-beauty/.
5. At this point, I want to clearly identify Dr. Don Hudson as a father of story thinking. I learned about these categories from him.
6. *Shalom* is the Hebrew word for "peace." It means more than congeniality or calmness. It is the pure absence of strife, struggle, and evil.
7. That means, "like Eden."
8. Usually. Stories are as unique as people, and while there are any number of exceptions to the rule, the rule is in place because the vast majority of stories follow this pattern. Don't get anxious if not every story "fits." All stories are unique yet all stories are similar. This is the beauty and complexity of story.
9. A phrase I attribute to my training from Dan Allender.
10. A fantastic treatment of living between these two trees can be found in Rob Bell's Nooma video called, "Trees." Check it out. https://www.christianbook.com/trees-003-rob-bell/pd/DV2256-CP.
11. Dénouement is often used in literary language and is the French word for the ending of the story. It has etymological ties to meaning "coming untied." It is the resolution at the end, when the twisted nature of the story unravels once again.
12. Because of this, we have named our ministry Restoration Project. Restoration is God's purpose in the world—to restore all things to what He originally intended.

## 6. WHAT'S YOUR STORY? PART II

1. "Highland Park Fire," Colorado Encyclopedia, last modified November 02, 2022, https://coloradoencyclopedia.org/article/high-park-fire

2. NIV.
3. NIV.
4. Among many others throughout the biblical text.
5. Eph. 1:4, NIV.
6. Eph. 2:10, NIV.
7. C.S. Lewis, *The Lion the Witch and the Wardrobe* (New York: Macmillan, 1950), 75. Again, I can't help but refer to *The Chronicles of Narnia*. C.S. Lewis and J.R.R. Tolkien will forever be my poetic heroes. One day I've promised myself to make a holy pilgrimage to The Eagle and Child, the pub where their informal literary group "The Inklings," consisting of Christians and non-Christians alike, met to discuss their views of the world.
8. C.S. Lewis, *The Weight of Glory: And Other Addresses* (New York: HarperCollins, 2001) 26.
9. "The Lion King," imbd.com, https://www.imdb.com/title/tt0110357/characters/nm0000469.
10. See Eph. 3:15-21.
11. I am forever indebted to my friend and mentor, Dr. Dan Allender, for these insights into the original markings of God's glory on humanity. His teachings pepper almost every aspect of my thoughts, career, theology, and pursuits.
12. Heb. 11:13-16, NIV.
13. Exod. 33:18-23.
14. C.S. Lewis, *The Weight of Glory: And Other Addresses* (New York: HarperCollins, 2001) 26.
15. Chris Bruno, *Sage: A Man's Guide Into His Second Passage* (Fort Collins, CO: Restoration Project, 2022).

## 7. HOW TO ENGAGE A MAN'S STORY

1. Sorry to anyone named Gary. I'm sure you are a great guy.
2. Martin Luther King Jr., "The Nobel Peace Prize 1964," NobelPrize.org, Accessed April 17, 2023, https://www.nobelprize.org/prizes/peace/1964/king/lecture/.
3. Matt. 18:20, NIV.
4. Curt Thompson, *The Soul of Shame: Retelling the Stories We Believe About Ourselves* (Downers Grove: IL: InterVarsity Press, 2015), 138.
5. As an example, think about how one might have pity on another experiencing homelessness. There is a level of tenderness toward that person, but there is no stepping into their struggle with a sense of connectedness to their story. And the power difference remains as you drive away with your latte. Pity is an *I - It* interaction.
6. "Brene Brown on Empathy," youtube.com, December 10, 2013, https://youtu.be/1Evwgu369Jw.
7. NIV.
8. NIV.
9. Always feel free to reach out to my team at ReStory Counseling. We have a plethora of care options available, including intensives, therapy, storywork coaching, spiritual direction, etc. You can find us at www.restory.life.

## 8. PAIN

1. Game. To be honest, at this stage in my life, I truly viewed all of this as a game. A young man in my mid-20s, I was on the adventure of a lifetime. Conquering language, living sacrificially, bringing the gospel to unreached people...this was it! I sat directly in the middle of what I call the "Warrior Man" stage of a man's life. See my book *Sage: A Man's Guide Into His Second Passage* for my take on these stages.
2. Addictions have both a physical and an emotional element. Whatever the addiction, there is always an "ahhh, that feels good" kind of response, and this is both a physical release (think drugs, alcohol, orgasm, adrenaline, etc.) and an emotional release. The emotional component involves a separation from reality, where numbing the pain with action feels like a better choice than facing it.
3. This violence includes everything from the insidious nature of harm or any form of abuse (physical, emotional, verbal, sexual, spiritual, etc.), to "acceptable" violence, such as extreme sports, adrenaline junkies, career-ladder-climbers, etc. Violence of any kind reduces a man to a less-than-human existence. Strength is manly. Violence is primal.
4. For an excellent treatment of man's struggle with passivity, I recommend the following book: *Silence of Adam: Becoming Men of Courage in a World of Chaos* by Larry Crabb, Don Hudson, and Al Andrews. So much more can be said about man's plight with passivity, but that is for another book.
5. Richard Rohr, *Adam's Return: The Five Promises of Male Initiation*. (New York: Crossroad Publishing Company, 2004), 37.
6. Rohr, 39.
7. In fact, our bodies have pain suppressors called *endorphins*. Commonly known as the "runner's high," these chemicals are released into our bloodstream to reduce the painful experience of running long distances or exercising strenuously. Research has shown that the presence of these endorphins in our bloodstream also affects our emotional responses to difficult or painful situations. This is why doctors and therapists tell depressed or anxious patients to get exercise. God made our bodies as holistic systems.
8. Gen. 2:19.
9. Rohr, 47; italics added.
10. Dan Allender said this often throughout my training as a therapist.
11. Excerpts from Matt. 26:36-46, NIV.
12. Over the last several decades, "men's groups" have come to mean "accountability groups," where sin and sin management have been the focus of the discussion. While I believe that men can and should work together to help avoid sinful choices, I am firmly against the traditional notion of accountability groups. True relationship, true friendship, true brotherhood is about *journeying* together, not just about answering prescribed sin-questions. In this way, I believe the church has aided in the diminishing of what male friendship was intended to be. What our hearts really need are brothers.

## 9. NEED

1. Did you catch that I even threw in there "supposed," not believing the honesty of a man who *does* bring a need to another?
2. 1 Sam. 20:1-4, NIV.
3. It would do you well to study the friendship between David and Jonathan. Check out 1 Samuel 18 and 20, 2 Samuel 1 and 9. I believe most men would deeply benefit from learning how to speak boldly and tenderly with one another.
4. Much of what is deemed "men's ministry" is really a misnomer. Its focus is on sin management—keeping you in line so your sinful nature does not get the best of you. It's often about creating external structures intended to corral the internal beast that apparently lives in the mind, heart, and groin of every man. Now, I do believe that men need one another to avoid doing stupid things, but to minimize the relationship to "keeping one another accountable" is paramount to committing relational suicide. It doesn't work in the long haul and keeps men from genuine friendship. How's that for a little tirade?
5. What his exact words were I don't completely remember, but I do remember the distinct feeling of being pinned to the wall with nowhere to go. He saw right through me and called me to something more. *That's* what I remember.

## 10. BLESSING

1. At the risk of sounding completely crude, I call this sort of male-male comparison "dick measuring." It is the constant evaluation of my manhood versus his, my character versus his, and, therefore, my perceived value versus his. If I can outdo him, I rank higher. Otherwise, I am but a smaller and less masculine version of man than him.
2. Lewis, *Lion, the Witch and the Wardrobe*, 75.
3. From EWTN, the Global Catholic Network. https://www.ewtn.com/catholicism/saints/teresa-of-calcutta-13641.
4. Prov. 18:21, NIV
5. Prov. 16:24, NIV
6. Prov. 12:18, NIV
7. Prov. 18:4, New King James Version
8. Prov. 15:1
9. *Spider-Man*. 2002. [film] Directed by S. Raimi. USA: Columbia Pictures Corporation & Marvel Enterprises.
10. NIV.

## EPILOGUE: WHAT'S NEXT?

1. Much more could be said here, and I refer you to Henry Cloud's excellent book, *Necessary Endings: The Employees, Businesses, and Relationships That All of Us Have to Give Up in Order to Move Forward*.
2. NIV.

# INTRODUCTION TO SAGE

The subterranean tremors began to shake each of our lives in ways we did not understand. We felt the tectonic shifts deep within and somehow recognized the call to a new adventure, a new season, a new exploration of our lives as men. When we were younger, we may have understood this as a beckoning towards a higher mountain to climb, a steeper slope to ski, a more impossible business to start, or a greater promotion to attain. But now, at midlife, each of us knew this was altogether different.

Something psychological happens in a man's life when he crosses over the 40-year-old threshold. He wakes up to his limitations with a keen awareness the half-time show is about to start, and the morning of his life will soon turn towards afternoon. There is just as much behind as there is ahead, and he must reckon with the fact that midlife has arrived.

Thresholds must be marked, celebrated, and remembered. As John O'Donohue says, "A threshold is not a simple boundary; it is a frontier that divides two different territories, rhythms, and atmospheres." Choosing to live as intentional fathers, our small brotherhood of men knew our sons needed us to usher them over the first threshold men face from boyhood to manhood through a rite of passage process we came to call the *Man Maker Project*. Together, we attended to the hearts of our boys, answering their core questions, *"Am I a man? Do I have what it takes?"* with a resounding *"Yes!"* And while our boys have mostly made this first passage, truth be told, we all know boys do not instantly become men. It takes years.

For the four of us, as the soul-tremors grew louder and stronger and more insistent, we found *ourselves* at a new threshold of manhood, a second passage, one we knew we needed to cross. This next journey would require an equal amount of ritual, intention, and reflection. And so, together with three of my closest friends, Greg Daley, Bart Lillie, and Shae McCowen, we set out on an epic pilgrimage to Scotland in search of our own selves. We called it our *Second Half* journey.

We believe the three core conditions of life-changing moments are *experience, story, and blessing*. Therefore, Greg and I partnered up to craft a meaningful journey that paired physical adventure with soulful content. As a result, we canoed, kayaked, hiked, and toured distillery after distillery, all while inviting reflection, story, and mutual pursuit of each other's hearts. And while it began with a once-in-a-lifetime physical journey to the Scottish Highlands, the crossing of the spiritual and psychological threshold continues for each of us even years later. It is our second passage into manhood, into the second half, one that far too many men resist, neglect, or deny.

As a therapist and leader of a men's ministry organization, I have spent countless hours with men at all stages of the masculine journey: adolescent boys who long for a father to lead them, notice them, and bless them for who they are and not what they do; young men in their 20's first embracing the vigor of their lives as men as they pursue work and women, pushing the limits of their daring and power; guys in their 30's, grappling with increased responsibility at home and work, facing what it means to be faithful husband, intentional father, and adult son; men in their 40's and 50's, wondering what life is really about, realizing the prescribed formulas of the world and Church do not actually yield the promised results; and men in their 60's, 70's and 80's, who find themselves regretful, lonely, and pining for days gone by. With each of these men, I have experienced a deep inner struggle to orient themselves in the man-life God has given them. No one -- not even one -- has ever said, "I have arrived."

We must consider manhood as a journey, not a destination. Often, I ask men, "When did you become a man?" Answers to this question are all over the map, including, "when I left home" or "when I got my first job" or "when I had sex for the first time" or "when I got my driver's license" or "when I became a father." Again, no one has ever said, "I'm still becoming a man." The fact is, we are all still becoming men, because we are still discovering the mystery of who God made us to be, and why. The manhood journey is, however, cyclical rather than linear, and the closer we come to the end, we find ourselves once again at the beginning. "It calls us both backward and forward, to our foundation and our future, at the same time." To cross the second threshold, we must be prepared to go deeper and in reverse to recover those parts of us that have remained exiled, forgotten, lost, or never fully known.

There are four primary movements in a man's life: 1) when he is born; 2) when he crosses the threshold from boy to man; 3) when he recovers his True Self and crosses the threshold to the second half; and 4) when he dies. We have very little influence on our own physical beginning and ending. Birth and death are ruled by forces beyond us (though we do everything we can to gain God-like control). The two movements in which we consciously and purposefully *participate* are the crossing of the two thresholds, the passages from boy to man and the return of the man to the boy. While I have written about the first passage elsewhere, my task here is to explore the depths and challenges of the second passage, and what it means to enter and exist in the second half.

While I have a deep love and affection for women, and I believe women could benefit from what I have offered here, my primary audience is men. Certainly, there are many similarities between men and women when it comes to the first and second halves of our lives. However, as a man and as a leader of men's work, it is my focus and task to come alongside women in the *recovery* of their men. When we recognizing the unique value God has placed on humanity *as men* and *as women* we discover a more complete understanding of God's image. May the words here provide nourishment for whoever finds them.

Personally, I am on the front end of this life transition. Though the epic second half journey to Scotland took place years ago, as I sit today and write, I am a young 49 years old. I do not have the experience and tenure of being in my 60's, 70's, or 80's. The voices of these sages rings loudly in my ears, and I cherish their thoughts, words, and wisdom both for this work and for my own journey. I have always endeavored to live life out loud, to share my reflections and experiences with men I consider my contemporaries. My hope is to give words to the crucible of midlife and the first steps into the second half, and to offer hope and direction to men who are just a few years behind me.

As both a theologian and psychologist, I find both streams to be filled with refreshing waters, complementary in their insights, and suitable for guidance and soul-care. As a follower of Jesus, I look to him for life and existence and sustenance. Nothing exists, even myself, without the benevolent generosity of the Creator. I exist because he does.

Knowing a pilgrimage is a "physical journey with a spiritual destination," to write this book I have once again embarked on an epic expedition, this time to the far western coast of Ireland. In January. Alone. I sit within feet of the most westerly shores of Europe, coastlines where the rage of the winter sea breaks violently and constantly against the rugged cliffs of this ancient Celtic island. Rain is a forever companion here, and the crackle of the fire a constant reminder of God's warming presence. Whereas I came to the Isles several years ago with my friends, *this time* I knew I needed to come by myself. No one can help me recover my boy, the ultimate mission of the second half. That is my mission, and I must do it alone. And as you will see, it is the charge of every second half man.

*The task of the first passage is to find the man within the boy, and call him forth.*

*The task of the second passage is to find the boy within the man, and bring him home.*

I have divided this work into three main parts:

In Part 1, I set forth a vision for the Second Half Man, exploring God's purposes for this second passage, and the men he has designed us to become. We will reflect on the biblical understanding of "elder," and survey history and cultures to understand the Sage as the pinnacle of God's masculine design. And we will consider the devastating impact our world experiences when men merely grow old without becoming Sages.

In Part 2, we will explore the vital parts of a man's first half, uncovering the important stages through which a man must pass before he can cross the threshold of the second half. We will discuss the first passage from boy to man, and rediscover the divine masterpiece written into the narrative of our lives. I will help you identify your *projections* and your *personas*, two ways we survive in our first half that cannot accompany us across the second threshold. We will explore the shaky ground of midlife, and then end by recognizing the importance of coming to the end of ourselves before we take the first steps into the second half.

In Part 3, we will orient ourselves to the six hallmark characteristics of the Sage, including settled contentment, spacious hospitality, generous spirituality, the crucible of suffering, and the move from loneliness to solitude. We end with the culmination of the journey as the Sage welcomes home the boy within the man.

As G.K. Chesterton says, "We are all under the same mental calamity; we have all forgotten our names. We have all forgotten what we really are." On this journey into the second half, let us answer the call to remember our God-given identity, purpose, and meaning.

Let's bring our boys home.

———

*Sage* is available for purchase on Amazon.com

Chris Bruno received a master of arts in speech from Northwestern University and a master of arts in counseling psychology from The Seattle School of Theology and Psychology. He is the co-founder and CEO of Restoration Project, a ministry devoted to helping men recover their hearts by healing their wounds, knowing God, and restoring the world. He is a licensed professional counselor and the founder and CEO of ReStory® Counseling, leading a diverse and collaborative team of storywork counselors around the country. He is the author of *Man Maker Project: A Father's Guide for Initiating His Son Into Manhood* and *Sage: A Man's Guide Into His Second Passage*.

Chris has been married to Beth for 28 years, and they have three mostly adult children. After spending the better part of a decade in missions in the Near East, they settled in his home state of Colorado. Their love for travel permeates their home and dinnertime conversations, and a good adventure is always in the works.

Made in the USA
Columbia, SC
08 January 2024